The Hollywood Murder Casebook

Other books by Michael Munn, published by Robson Books

KIRK DOUGLAS
CHARLTON HESTON

The Hollywood Murder Casebook

Michael Munn

St. Martin's Press
New York

For Debbie—who wanted the facts

THE HOLLYWOOD MURDER CASEBOOK. Copyright © 1987 by Michael Munn.
All rights reserved. Printed in the United States of America. No part of this
book may be used or reproduced in any manner whatsoever without
written permission except in the case of brief quotations embodied in
critical articles or reviews. For information, address St. Martin's Press, 175
Fifth Avenue, New York, N.Y. 10010.

Library of Congress Cataloging-in-Publication Data

Munn, Michael.
        The Hollywood murder casebook / by Michael Munn.
            p.   cm.
        "A Thomas Dunne book."
        ISBN 0-312-01443-0 : $15.95
        1. Murder—California—Los Angeles—Case studies.   2. Moving
-picture actors and actresses—California—Los Angeles—Case
studies.   3. Hollywood (Los Angeles, Calif.)   I. Title.
HV6535.U63L76   1988
364.1′523′097949—dc19   87-27101
                                                                    CIP

First published in Great Britain by Robson Books Ltd.

First U.S. Edition

10   9   8   7   6   5   4   3   2   1

Contents

List of Illustrations

From Shoot-outs in the West to Arbuckle in Court

THIS BOOK IS a collection of unique tales of murder – unique because they could only have happened in the way that they happened in or around Hollywood. Not a State of America, not even a city, but a suburb of Los Angeles, Hollywood has been, for more than seventy years, an institution, a symbol of American film-making, the Mecca of motion pictures. The very word 'Hollywood' has come to personify everything that one imagines the motion picture industry to be built upon – wealth, power, glamour, talent, star quality. They are all elements which make this book of true murder cases uniquely Hollywood.

This is certainly not a legal tract, an official report, or a police file, but a journalistic investigation that grew out of a gradual and peculiar experience, through intense research into Hollywood lives and careers, of 'getting to know' film-makers and movie stars who, though many are now dead, somehow touched me through their lives and experiences. Delving deeply through material and discovering the personalities behind the names of such people as Mabel Normand, Thomas Ince, William Randolph Hearst, William Desmond Taylor, Sal Mineo, Marilyn Monroe and countless others, inevitably produced a certain amount of empathy, sympathy and sometimes antipathy towards them. One can't help but feel that some have been maligned and some guiltless people implicated in crime, while others have perhaps been absolved through corruption. That is why some of these cases may not be proven murders, but still need investigation. In such cases, I do not pretend to expose the absolute truth and reach definite conclusions; rather I explore all the known evidence, examine testimonies critically and raise questions that may help the reader to evaluate each case. These are matters for the amateur sleuth – for instance, the mysteries which still surround the unsolved murders of film director William Desmond Taylor and actress Thelma Todd.

Included also are crimes of passion and court-room dramas featuring star witnesses such as John Wayne and Lana Turner. There are cases of pure brutality that have in latter years clearly typified our violent times – the slaying of the original *Ben-Hur*, the ritualistic slaughter of Sharon Tate and her drug-cultured friends, and the senseless stabbing of one-time heart-throb Sal Mineo.

Each case speaks clearly for itself, yet as a collection a story is told of a Hollywood that has never really been seen before. To get a clear perspective on that story, we must begin at the very beginning of Hollywood, when the gun really did rule and the threat to lives was an occupational hazard.

Hollywood was a genuine part of the old Wild West. Even as motion picture companies were migrating from East Coast to West, it was a lawless frontier town.

It began simply as a ranch to which a real estate man, Harvey Henderson Wilcox, and his wife Deida retired in 1886. The West at that time had still not been completely won, but civilization was advancing, and in 1891 Wilcox began dividing the land around Hollywood ranch and distributing maps to real estate agents. He envisaged his ranch blossoming into a town, and by 1903 it had grown into a small village, retaining the name Hollywood. In 1910 it was annexed to the city of Los Angeles to avail itself of the city's water supply and sewerage system.

Back East, a powerful and illegal Trust began operating, calling itself The Motion Picture Patents Company (MPPC). Edison and Biograph, two of the biggest film companies of that time, were the sole stockholders and were allied with Vitagraph, Armat, Essanay, Kalem, Selig, Kleine, Lubin, Pathé and Méliès. They claimed to own all rights to produce, distribute and exhibit films in the United States, and any independent who wished to make pictures and show them to the public had to pay fees and royalties for the use of cameras, projectors and any other equipment covered by their patents. It was the beginning of the last great Wild West showdown.

Independent companies began an exodus from New York,

then the centre of American film production, and headed for California. The New York Motion Picture Company opened a studio in Edendale in 1909, and two years later Vitagraph came to Santa Monica. Also in 1911 the Nestor Studios became the very first movie studio to open in Hollywood. Other companies continued to set up operations in California, partly to take advantage of the perpetual sunshine and also to escape the MPPC who now reverted to violent means to put a stop to these independents making movies without paying their fees.

Gunmen paid by the Trust began arriving on trains from the East, burning down studios and shooting up camera equipment. There was no law to speak of to protect the Californian film-makers, so they took the law into their own hands. This led to inevitable shoot-outs, and making movies became a dangerous business.

The last few big cattle drives were pushing a dusty trail across the plains. Cowboys, old-time lawmen and redundant posses converged on the areas in California where moving pictures were being made. They became extras in cowboy films and were paid five dollars a day. But they weren't paid just for acting. Their talents as gunmen were put to good use and, armed with Winchesters, they fought off the gangsters whom the Trust continued to send out West.

For a while the independents fought under one banner – the Motion Picture Distributing and Sales Company – and were led by its founder, Carl Laemmle. But that broke into two factions, the breakaway company calling itself the Universal Film Manufacturing Company which behaved just like the Trust. It hired its own gunmen to sneak back to New York and attempt to recover what it regarded as its own property from the remainder of the MPDSC, the New York Motion Picture Company which still had its main base on the East coast. When the people at the New York laboratory heard of an impending attack, they mustered armed guards, and a gun battle ensued.

The Universal people also sent armed men to Los Angeles to besiege Inceville, the studio which Tom Ince, who specialized in westerns, had built. He had a whole army of real cowboys and they were waiting when the Universal gunslingers arrived. Ince gave orders that anyone attempting to get in the main gate was to be shot. The Universal gunmen retreated.

At that time the studios surrounded Hollywood, though very few were actually in it, and so the budding town was little touched by the range war between East and West. Hollywood was certainly the most attractive of the Los Angeles suburbs and the movie people set up home there or simply lived in the Hollywood Hotel. Many of them refrained from buying property and stayed in the hotel because they really had no idea that they were creating an art form that would endure.

The actors and studios were not at that time caught up in any star system, and salaries were by no means exorbitant. But with people living in such close proximity, it was inevitable that relationships would form, strengthening the Hollywood movie community. By and large they behaved themselves, and in those pre-World War One years there was not a whiff of scandal in the community itself. Then, in 1911, a Japanese gardener went crazy because of all the noise that emanated from the Selig Studio in Edendale. He went completely berserk and in a rage went to the studio and killed director Francis Boggs.

Cecil B. De Mille wasn't taking any chances when he arrived in Hollywood in 1913 to film *The Squaw Man*. He came packing a revolver. Initially he had gone to Flagstaff, Arizona, to make his film, but had arrived in the middle of a cattleman-sheepman war and the bullets were flying. So he got back on the train and went to Hollywood.

The Trust noted De Mille's obvious determination to remain out West, and they made numerous death threats to him. One evening, while he was riding home through Cahuenga Pass, he was caught in an ambush. A gunman was hiding in the bushes and opened fire on De Mille. The director felt a bullet whistle past his head, but arrived home unhurt though shaken. But he, and the others, refused to give in, and eventually the law was able to close down the Trust, leaving film-makers free to film wherever they wanted to. That war was at an end.

But there was still a sense of lawlessness about Hollywood, emphasized by the presence of cowboys all over the place. One such man was Yakima Jim, a desperate and dangerous cowpoke who was always trying to provoke the other cowboys into fights.

His big mistake was in picking on Tom Bay, a desperado from Oklahoma who had killed a man there. Now he was a movie stuntman, but not one to take Yakima Jim's jibes. When Jim pulled a knife and threatened to slice Bay's belly open, Bay whipped out his six-shooter and shot Yakima Jim dead.

It was that kind of town. But with the patents war over, motion picture production in and around Hollywood flourished and the community grew at an alarming rate. Movies were the country's most popular form of entertainment. Audiences flocked in their millions every week to see silent pictures, and movie stars who had previously been anonymous became known by their names. It was then that the studios realized just what valuable commodities their actors were. So began the star system with performers coming under contract and tied exclusively to one studio or another and being paid enormous sums of money.

The Teens of Hollywood were called the halcyon days. The stars earned fortunes which had to be spent one way or another. Some, in an effort to find new highs in their lives, turned to cocaine, or 'joy powder' as it was known. Opium was sold openly and legitimately over the counter. The people of Hollywood could get high without fear of arrest, and studios administered drugs of every kind to their stars to pep them up or calm them down. Even in those 'halcyon days', movie stars were becoming drug addicts.

It was in 1920 that drugs and alcohol were outlawed through Prohibition, but already too many of Hollywood's brightest stars were on the road to destruction, and it was only a matter of time before something broke. And it did, in that same year.

Beautiful actress Olive Thomas, wife of actor Jack Pickford (brother of Mary Pickford), was found dead of a drugs overdose in a Paris hotel. Her studio had labelled and sold her as the 'Ideal American Girl'. Now everyone knew that the Ideal American Girl had been a junkie. What they didn't know at that time, though, was that Jack Pickford, 'The Ideal American Boy', was a drunk, and in years to come would waste away from alcoholism.

That same year, another popular young star, Bobby Harron, died of a gun-shot wound. His studio frantically concocted a story that he had accidently dropped a loaded revolver which had gone off when it hit the floor. But rumours that he had shot himself persisted, many of his peers maintaining that it had been suicide.

Such stories kept the headlines hot, and church ministers and women's groups began to get uneasy about the apparent immorality which seemed rampant in Hollywood. So far, though, there was nothing tangible they could rebuke.

Then in 1921 something happened which affected the whole of Hollywood.

Roscoe 'Fatty' Arbuckle was, in the public's eyes, second only to Charlie Chaplin. They loved his sense of vulgar fun, and with his two-reel comedies making a fortune, Adolph Zukor, the head of Paramount, signed him to a three-million-dollar contract to make feature-length pictures.

To celebrate, Roscoe held a party at the St Francis Hotel in San Francisco on Labour Day – 5 September 1921. To help the party go with a swing, he had allocated a good supply of bootleg liquor to ply his fifty or so guests with.

Four days later, one of the guests, Virginia Rappe, died in the Wakefield Sanatorium. Maude Delmont, another guest, went to the police and made an astonishing claim: Roscoe Arbuckle had raped Virginia Rappe and had killed her with his immense weight.

When District Attorney Matthew Brady, who was seeking re-election that year, heard of Delmont's accusation, he immediately seized upon this opportunity to win votes. He announced to the press that he would convict Arbuckle of Miss Rappe's death.

The world's headlines screamed the shocking news: ARBUCKLE HELD FOR MURDER.

There was a sudden furore in America. Cinemas withdrew Fatty Arbuckle films, and religious and women's organizations campaigned to have Arbuckle's career immediately terminated. They had already judged him, and the trial hadn't even begun.

Adolph Zukor stopped Arbuckle's salary and put a total embargo on his films. With this sudden outcry against the monster comedian, Zukor decided to do all he could to placate the paying customers, and he forbade any of his stars to stand as character witnesses for Arbuckle.

A number of witnesses were put under close guard by the DA's office to prevent, they said, any intimidation by lawyers. In fact, any intimidation was to come from Brady himself as he began to realize the one great truth of the matter – Maude Delmont, his star witness, was a liar. Consequently, he refused to allow her to take the stand, even though she was the one person who had made the claim that Arbuckle had raped and murdered Rappe.

Brady told the world, 'This is first-degree murder. We don't feel a man like Arbuckle can pull stuff like this in San Francisco and get away with it.'

Brady had a powerful ally. William Randolph Hearst was a newspaper tycoon of unbelievable power and influence. In this scandalous case he saw ammunition to boost circulation. He ordered his newspapers to wage war on Arbuckle, going so far as to fake photographs of Arbuckle behind bars.

In an effort to prove that Arbuckle had indeed dragged Virginia Rappe to his bedroom and, despite her pitiful screams, brutally raped her, Brady resorted to threatening the other witnesses and suppressing evidence which would damage his case. He was suddenly as big a star as Arbuckle and the public looked to him as some kind of hero, protecting them from the loose-living drunkards of Hollywood. The whole film community was, in a sense, on trial, but it was Arbuckle who had to stare humiliation in the face.

The jury, however, were not taken in by all the excitement, and they suspected something was wrong. They succeeded in reducing the charge to one of manslaughter.

Slowly but surely, as the trial progressed, much of the truth came to light regarding the victim and Maude Delmont.

Delmont was known as 'Madame Black', and she specialized in organizing pretty and easy girls for parties. She coaxed her girls to make claims that prominent film-makers or actors had tried to rape them, and then threaten legal action. They usually earned for themselves, and for Madame Black, a tidy sum.

Meanwhile, Hearst's newspapers printed Virginia Rappe's life story, portraying her as a poor innocent victim.

Rival newspapers dug out the real truth, though. Rappe had been a model in Chicago, and had come to Hollywood in the hope of becoming an actress. Mack Sennett, the producer of some of the funniest comedies around, and discoverer of Arbuckle and Chaplin, gave her a number of bit parts. During her time with Sennett, she took the opportunity of sleeping with half the Sennett company.

She had a passionate affair with director Henry 'Pathé' Lehrman, but when Sennett discovered that Lehrman and many of his employees had contracted a venereal disease from Rappe, he fired her and had the studio fumigated. Out of work, Rappe turned to Maude Delmont, and became quite famous for stripping off at parties, and it was through Delmont that she came to be at Arbuckle's party.

She was also a drunk, even though she had been warned by a doctor that she should lay off alcohol. At Arbuckle's party she had consumed so much bootleg liquor that she became totally paralytic.

A doctor had carried out an examination on Rappe's body to see if she had been sexually attacked. The doctor concluded that she had not, but Brady suppressed this evidence. At the trial, though, the jury heard that Virginia had had several abortions and suffered from VD.

When the jury retired, the majority were in favour of acquittal. But one woman, a friend of Brady, refused to acquit Arbuckle and insisted on his guilt.

A second trial ensued, and Zukor brought in another lawyer (he hadn't completely abandoned Arbuckle). But the whole film industry now felt that they had to do something to save their business, no matter what happened to Arbuckle. They hastily formed the Motion Picture Producers and Distributors of America Inc. and assigned the postmaster-general, Will H. Hays, to lead them in combating immorality in Hollywood.

While this was in progress the second trial almost proved a disaster for Arbuckle. The defence had been so sure that they had their case all sewn up that they didn't bother to call Arbuckle to the stand.

With neither Delmont nor Arbuckle giving testimony, the given evidence became very conflicting, especially under Brady's corrupt scrutiny. The jury favoured a verdict of guilty this time, but there were some who held out for his acquittal, and a third trial had to be conducted.

Taking no chances, the defence put their case forward with tremendous impact, and finally Roscoe Arbuckle was acquitted and the jury offered an apology to Arbuckle. They said:

Acquittal is not enough for Roscoe Arbuckle. We feel that a great injustice has been done him. There was not the slightest proof adduced to connect him in any way with the commission of a crime. He was manly throughout the case and told a straightforward story which we all believed. We wish him success and hope that the American people will take the judgement of fourteen men and women that Roscoe Arbuckle is entirely innocent and free of all blame.

The next scandal really threatened to sink the film industry once and for all; it was Hollywood's most baffling murder, and with it we open our Hollywood murder casebook.

William Desmond Taylor: The All-star Murder mystery

NO ONE COULD have known his exact thoughts, but William Desmond Taylor had a great deal on his mind as he sat in quiet contemplation in his study. His last visitor had left some ten minutes ago and he was alone in his bungalow court apartment on Alvarado Street in the quiet Los Angeles suburb of Westlake.

It was the night of 1 November 1922. Roscoe 'Fatty' Arbuckle was just two days away from the close of his second trial, and the whole of Hollywood was on a knife edge; few felt its razor sharpness more than Taylor.

He was forty-five. His greased-down black hair had just a touch of grey at the temples. He was still a trim, handsome man and enjoyed the status of being the top film director at Famous Players-Lasky, a subsidiary of Paramount. Taylor's immediate boss was Charles Eyton, general manager of Famous Players-Lasky, but the man who pulled the strings was the head of Paramount, Adolph Zukor. For Zukor, the Arbuckle scandal had been his most searing nightmare. The whole industry was sweltering under the weight of the anti-Hollywood feeling that was sweeping the country. Paramount, where Arbuckle was under contract, was a veritable battle HQ which shook heavily under the onslaught from leaders of the Church and other organizations, who rebuked Hollywood for inciting the Youth of America to debauchery.

Taylor found himself in the front line. His prestige in the industry and the respect in which he was held by his peers was such that he was elected president of the Motion Picture Directors Association (MPDA), and as such he was under direct instructions from the Hollywood hierarchy to clean up Hollywood.

The MPDA with Taylor at its head had the task of fumigating the movie industry and making it suitable for the public. Taylor had spoken out in response to those who claimed that the people responsible were not doing enough to tighten Hollywood's morals:

> I have listened with amazement to the charges of these ministers that we are debauching the morals of the youth of this city. We have not been cleaning house for very long – just a few months. In those few months we have cleaned house with a vengeance.

In the eyes of the public he was a crusader, and his image was enhanced by his claim to have been an officer in the British Army. He kept his uniform at his bungalow apartment, and even had photographs of himself in military attire distributed. He maintained the image by arraying himself constantly in jodhpurs and shining riding boots both on and off film sets. He cut a dashing figure.

The rumour in Hollywood was that he was a homosexual, and the gossip flared when he acquired the services of a homosexual negro butler, Henry Peavey, who loved to crochet delicate little doilies.

But few people knew the real William Desmond Taylor. Among those who did was Adolph Zukor and a few close lady friends. Taylor had also had a valet, Edward F. Sands, but Taylor fired him, he said, for forging cheques and stealing clothes and jewellery.

With Sands no longer in his employ, then, his last visitor of the night gone and Peavey enjoying his night off, Taylor was completely alone. He sat back in his chair.

Suddenly he was no longer alone. Standing in the open door of his study stood a figure dressed in a long coat. A muffler was around the chin; a cap was pulled low over the eyes. Taylor found himself staring down the barrel of a .38-calibre revolver.

He suddenly lurched out of his chair, turning towards a small desk that stood by the window. His back was now to the intruder. The gun fired twice, pumping two bullets into Taylor's back. His hand caught the chair, knocking it off balance. He fell in front of the desk, the chair toppling on to his legs. He died face upwards with both eyes wide open and his arms outstretched.

The killer retreated from the bungalow, the face virtually hidden by the muffler and the cap. But from across the court the figure was watched from behind curtains. Mrs Faith Cole MacLean had heard what had sounded like a small explosion. Her curiosity had, as usual, got the better of her, and not for the first time that late evening, she peered out of her window. She knew who many of Taylor's visitors were, but this was someone unrecognizable. She watched the mysterious figure disappear from sight. Then she pulled her curtains shut and thought no more about it.

A high-pitched soprano voice caused Edna Purviance to stir in her bed. Her eyes, set in a pert, round and pretty face, flickered open. It was daylight, but very early.

The voice came louder, wailing disconsolately from outside. She rose from her bed, hardly looking at this time of the day like the glamorous leading lady of Chaplin's films. Looking out of her window she saw in the court Henry Peavey in a state of near hysteria.

'Dey've kilt massa! Dey've kilt massa!' he cried over and over. Then he ran down into Alvarado Street, still crying and carrying on. A few angry faces appeared at windows. Some told him to pipe down. But he continued to run up and down weeping and crying inconsolably, 'Dey've kilt massa!'

Meanwhile, Edna had quickly dressed and rushed over to Taylor's bungalow. In the study she found him, lying in a scarlet pool, staring lifelessly up at the ceiling. Quickly gathering her wits, she knew what had to be done. She rushed back to her own apartment and reached for the telephone.

But she didn't call the police.

The sleepy voice that answered her call belonged to Mabel Normand.

Mabel had the looks of a screen siren. Standing just five feet three inches, she possessed a generously proportioned body. Her black hair and brown saucer eyes were appealing enough to make numerous top Hollywood figures fall in love with her. Yet her talent on the screen was to make people laugh, and throughout the whole silent screen era she reigned as the finest of all movie comediennes. But off the screen, although her sense of humour always shone through, she was a wild, passionate woman, and her love affairs with members of the Hollywood hierarchy were not part of the public image of Mabel Normand.

She had, in fact, partnered Chaplin when he first started in films, and when she pursued her own successful course in feature films, he chose Edna Purviance, a secretary from San Francisco, to replace her.

Edna and Mabel were friends, and Edna knew that Mabel would want to know that Taylor was dead. Mabel was panic-stricken, and the first thought that flashed through her mind was to hightail it over to Taylor's bungalow. But another thought over-ruled it. She reached for the phone.

But she didn't call the police.

Charles Eyton answered, and Mabel told him the tragic news. Then she hung up and, fighting off tidal waves of fear and panic, she dressed and leapt into her limousine.

Eyton didn't waste a minute. He made a phone call.

But he didn't call the police.

In an instant he was relaying the shocking news to Adolph Zukor. The Paramount chief, just forty years of age and about the most influential and powerful man in Hollywood, was thunderstruck. But it was not through grief for his dead friend that his heart almost stopped. He ordered Eyton to meet him at Taylor's bungalow.

Meanwhile, Edna had put through another call.

But she didn't call the police.

The phone in Mary Miles Minter's home rang. But there was no answer. Edna had no idea where Mary, the demure heroine of so many Paramount pictures, could be. But she knew Mary would want to know of Taylor's death. In desperation, Edna phoned Mrs Charlotte Shelby, Mary's mother. Mrs Shelby insisted that she didn't know where her daughter was, but promised to break the news of Taylor's death to her at the first opportunity.

Another call was made from the vicinity of Alvarado Street. This time it was from an irate neighbour, and this time it did go through to the police department. His exact words to the sergeant on the desk were few: 'Come collect the crazy coon.'

A police car was soon rolling down Alvarado Street, the cops inside looking for the wailing negro. They spotted him running into the court where the bungalow apartments stood. They turned into the court and saw Peavey, still stricken with grief.

'Dey've kilt massa! Dey've kilt massa!' was all they could extract from him.

He pointed to the open door of Taylor's bungalow. Right outside were parked a number of cars. The cops went inside and there they were greeted by a bizarre sight.

Lying on the floor of the study was the body. Standing by the blazing fireplace was Adolph Zukor, feeding the flames with various papers. Scooping up bottles of bootleg liquor was Charles Eyton. Tearing the place apart was Mabel Normand. And standing and watching in stupefied silence was Edna Purviance.

The cops immediately put in a call to homicide, and before long the bungalow was swarming with detectives. The most obvious motive – robbery – was immediately ruled out. Still on Taylor's finger was his large 'lucky' diamond ring which he had worn since his first film, *The Diamond From the Sky*.

The body was photographed and an intensive search for clues got under way. Whatever Mabel Normand had been looking for so frantically, whatever had been destroyed by Adolph Zukor and Charles Eyton, enough evidence was unearthed by detectives not only to implicate a number of suspects, but also to fulfil Zukor's worst fears. And that was the discovery that William Desmond Taylor, who had been 'cleaning house' after the Arbuckle scandal, had failed to put his own house in order first.

A policeman, rummaging through one of Taylor's drawers, found a stack of binders. Removing them, he discovered they were nothing more than scenarios of some of Taylor's pictures. But there was something else hidden behind them, placed right at the bottom of the drawer so that a casual browser would not have found it.

It was a pile of photographs, and very quickly they became the subject of widespread interest among the whole squad. They were pornographic pictures featuring Taylor and a variety of easily identifiable women engaged in sexual gratification. Out of the window flew all the rumours that Taylor had been homosexual, and the news quickly spread that the man who had been 'cleaning house' was himself a perverted Lothario.

Several actresses were questioned, including Mabel Normand who was almost immediately cornered by police who wanted to know what she had been doing in Taylor's bungalow that very morning, engaged in such frenzied activity.

She freely admitted that she had been looking for letters that she had written to Taylor which, she said, she had not wanted to be read by outsiders.

'I admit this,' she said, 'but it was only for one purpose – to prevent terms of affection from being misconstrued.'

What exactly was there to misconstrue?

The question remained unanswered for a time as further items came to light, diverting the investigators away from Mabel, at least for a while.

One detective had come across a pornographic book, crudely entitled *White Stains*. As he picked it up, a letter fluttered from between its pages. A sweet perfume wafted from the delicate pink paper. The words on the letter read:

> Dearest –
> I love you – I
> love you – I
> love you — —
> XXXXXXXXX
>
> yours always!
> Mary

The letterhead was a printed logo: a large butterfly in the shape of an M. It was the well-known trademark of Mary Miles Minter.

According to Mrs Shelby, when she told Mary the news of Taylor's death, Mary broke down and wept loud and long, so distraught was she over the loss of one of her favourite directors who had guided her through some of her finest films. But by the time police arrived to question her, she had composed herself.

Mary had the sweetest face, prettier than Mary Pickford after whom she was fashioned, with long curly hair, usually hanging in ringlets. She was just twenty years old and had been a star since the age of six. Paramount had nurtured her demure, virginal image throughout her teenage years, and her huge eyes and slightly chubby figure accented the child-woman roles she specialized in. And, as was true with all the stars of that era, she was expected by the terms of her contract to carry her screen image into her own life. To do otherwise was to jeopardize a dazzling career.

When faced with the letter found in the pornographic book, Mary said, 'I did love him deeply and tenderly, with all the admiration a young girl gives to a man with the poise and position of Mr Taylor.'

She knew nothing about the book called *White Stains*; Taylor had placed the letter in its pages for reasons best known to himself. The letter was hardly passionate; indeed, in harmony with Mary's innocent screen image, her words seemed to express little more than an intense schoolgirl crush on an older teacher-figure. Much older, in fact – by twenty-five years. So far there was little to suggest more than an embarrassingly silly unrequited love. Mary's image had not been harmed.

As the search for clues continued, police dug up further evidence of Taylor's secret life. In a locked closet in his bedroom, a hoard of women's underwear was discovered. The majority of the garments were panties, and each item was tagged with the initials of the owner and the date on which they had been removed. Taylor, in whose hands the movie directors of Hollywood had placed all their hopes of regaining favour with the great American public, had ensured that his memories of days and nights of lust were kept vivid, not just with photographs of his lurid acts, but with a unique collection of souvenirs.

Among the lingerie was found an 'item' with the initials M.M.M. embroidered on it.

This 'item' has gone down in the history of Hollywood as being a flimsy, pink, silk nightie. However, veteran Hollywood columnist Adela Rogers St John, whose father was a highly respected lawyer in the Hollywood community in those roaring Twenties, wrote a book called *The Honeycomb*, revealing much of

Hollywood's secret life, in which she claimed that it was a pair of panties with the initials M.M.M. which had been found, and she also claimed that they were in her possession.

Whatever the 'item' was, the initials immediately implicated Mary Miles Minter, although she always maintained that what police had actually found was simply a handkerchief. It had come into Taylor's possession, she said, when she was trying one day to get a piece of grit out of her eye using her little lace hanky.

'Here,' said Taylor, 'take a real handkerchief, not that little dab of lace you have there.'

According to Mary, she kept Taylor's handkerchief and he kept hers which did have her initials on it. And, she says, that is what the police found.

A nightie, a pair of panties or a handkerchief? Whatever it was, it was enough to send reporters scuttling to their desks to reveal that Mary Miles Minter, America's other Sweetheart, had been having an affair with William Desmond Taylor.

The police were not interested in the gossip which their investigation inevitably produced, but they were looking for a murderer, and they didn't rule out the possibility that Taylor's love affairs and his death were connected.

Mrs Faith Cole MacLean was a most cooperative witness, and a very valuable one as the police discovered when they questioned neighbours. No one else seemed to have seen or heard anything.

'I wasn't sure then that it was a shot at all,' she told detectives about the events of the previous evening, 'but I distinctly heard an explosion. Then I glanced out of my window and I saw a man leaving the house and going down the walk. I *suppose* it was a man!

'It was dressed like a man, but, you know, funny looking. It was dressed in a heavy coat with a muffler around the chin and a cap pulled down over the eyes. But it walked like a woman – quick little steps and broad hips and short legs.'

Here at last was a worthwhile witness. Nobody else in the neighbourhood had anything to tell, not even Edna Purviance or the others found at the scene of the crime. The police became even more intrigued when Mrs MacLean revealed something else.

About ten minutes before the incident, Mrs MacLean had seen someone leave Taylor's apartment in a limousine: it was Mabel Normand.

Not only that, but Mary Miles Minter had also been to Taylor's bungalow that evening.

The police again turned their attention on Mabel, and she admitted that she had been there that night. She had been given a gift by Taylor: the latest volume of Freud.

Mabel and Mary went immediately to the top of the list of suspects. Mabel's letters were found tucked deep inside one of Taylor's riding boots, and her romantic involvement with Taylor was undeniable. Mary was already implicated. But they were not just members of Taylor's exclusive club with whom he satisfied his inexhaustible lusts: his affairs with Mabel and Mary were passionate and touched, at least, with genuine friendship. His affairs with the two stars had been running simultaneously, however, and, the police reasoned, were possibly causes of jealousy. Many a lover had been killed because of that passion.

There was another woman, it turned out, with whom Taylor was also having an affair, but she could answer no questions. She was Zelda Crosby, a writer at Famous Players-Lasky: shortly after Taylor's death, she killed herself.

As the list of suspects grew and the twilight world of Taylor's private life was illuminated, a portrait of the real William Desmond Taylor emerged, and the man was at last revealed.

His real name was William Cunningham Deane-Tanner. He came from County Cork in Ireland, and was born on 26 April 1877. His family had come to America and settled in New York where William and his younger brother Denis opened their own antique business.

William met and later married one of the Floradora Girls, a vaudeville act. The new Mrs Deane-Tanner gave birth to a little girl, and they were a handsome and happy little family. Then, inexplicably, Deane-Tanner disappeared, deserting his wife and child. It was as though he had vanished off the face of the earth.

Shortly after, William Desmond Taylor emerged on the West

Coast, making a living as a stage actor. He was an impressive, gentlemanly and charming character who boasted of having served as an officer in the British Army.

He arrived in Hollywood at a time when movies were in their infancy. Film directors were usually actors who had found that their talent was more evident behind the camera. Such men included D.W. Griffith and Cecil B. De Mille.

After just a few appearances in motion pictures, William Desmond Taylor landed his first directing job. It was a serial, *The Diamond From the Sky*, made by the American Film Company in 1915. It was in part directed by Jacques Jaccard, and had been intended to be a vehicle for Mary Pickford, who at that time was the biggest money-making star in the business. Famous Players had Pickford under contract, and the American Film Company tried to lure her over to their side with the promise of $4,000 a week. When she finally shook them off, they settled for her younger sister, Lottie Pickford.

Lottie and brother Jack had long lived in the shadow of Mary who, when she joined Biograph in 1909, ensured that both her brother and sister found work there too. When 'Little Mary', as she was known, went over to Laemmle's Independent Motion Picture Company, brother and sister went too at her insistence. And when Famous Players put America's Sweetheart under contract to them, they also had to settle for Lottie and Jack.

Without Mary, it's doubtful that either Lottie or Jack would ever have made names for themselves. Making *The Diamond From the Sky* was Lottie's biggest break, and her work on this, under William Desmond Taylor's direction, was for him the beginning of a long friendship and working association with all three Pickfords.

Taylor quickly established himself as a leading director and went to work for the Pallas company which, in 1916, was incorporated into Zukor's ever-growing Paramount complex. That same year Zukor's Famous Players merged with Lasky, and so Famous Players-Lasky became another successful subsidiary of Paramount. Now that Adolph Zukor had Mary Pickford in his powerful combo, he formed Artcraft Pictures Corporation for the sole purpose of packaging and distributing Mary Pickford vehicles.

Coming under Zukor's banner, Taylor usually found himself directing one Pickford or another, and helped Jack become a star in his own right in 1917 as *Tom Sawyer*. Robert Gordon played Huckleberry Finn, and the great success of the film prompted Taylor to reunite Pickford and Gordon in a sequel, *Huck and Tom*.

Taylor was fast establishing himself in the realm of wholesome family entertainment, and, intent on keeping him in that genre, Zukor had Taylor direct Mary Pickford for the first time in 1918 in *How Could You Jean?* followed quickly by *Johanna Enlists*.

Zukor now had quite a prestigious little ensemble of providers of innocent entertainment with the Pickfords and Taylor, and it became a full-time job for the publicity boys at Paramount to keep their names out of the scandal sheets. Zukor went so far as to insist that Mary Pickford was still an unmarried virgin, even though she was married to Owen Moore and committing adultery with Douglas Fairbanks Sr.

It didn't help that all three Pickfords liked to drink – Jack was a hopeless alcoholic. Ever since the death of his wife Olive Thomas from a drugs overdose, there had been the suspicion that he was also on drugs. All this, whether rumour or fact, had to be kept out of the public eye.

For Taylor, the image was far easier to maintain: as a director, his face was unknown by the public and he could go where he pleased. He frequented seedy little places around Los Angeles where it was said that effeminate men and masculine women gathered, and a selection of narcotics such as morphine, marijuana and opium were served on tea trolleys. These were the years of the Great World War, and people were more concerned with global events than with who did what in Hollywood, so that Taylor was able to go about largely unnoticed in his private Bohemian existence. But the war didn't last for ever.

In 1920 Taylor completed his famous trilogy of Huck and Tom pictures with *Huckleberry Finn*, only now Jack Pickford and Robert Gordon were a little too over-the-hill to portray the young scalawags of Mark Twain's books. A couple of unknown boy actors were found; Gordon Griffith as Tom and Lewis

Sargeant as Huck. Once again Taylor's reputation as a maker of family films was confirmed.

It was also the year when Mary Pickford left Zukor's employ and united with Fairbanks, Chaplin and D.W. Griffith to form their own company, United Artists. In an effort to fill the hole which Pickford left, Zukor signed up Mary Miles Minter to make films for Realart, yet another subsidiary of Paramount.

Taylor was the natural choice to direct some of Mary's films, beginning with the classic, *Anne of Green Gables*, (Her co-star in the film was Paul Kelly, who was later to spend two years in prison for the manslaughter of stage actor Ray Raymond.) Audiences loved the combination of Minter and Taylor, and further films followed in quick succession throughout 1920. What the public didn't see, however, was the sight of the eminently respectable and dignified Taylor seducing the seemingly innocent Mary Miles Minter in his bungalow apartment.

Neither did they know of the string of screen beauties who allowed themselves to be used by Taylor for his own bizarre gratification. He had valet Edward F. Sands take photographs of himself and his sexual conquests, displaying not so much voyeurism as narcissism. Among these seemingly willing models were some of the screen's best-known actresses, although the police, or possibly the studio heads, succeeded in keeping their identities secret. But what could possibly have possessed these screen goddesses to run such risks, surely knowing that the discovery of such pictures might well have ended their careers?

Certainly Taylor, like almost every other actor and film-maker of that time, kept a supply of bootleg liquor. Prohibition was not enough to keep dry those who could afford illicit booze. Did Taylor simply ply these women with enough drink that they willingly subjected themselves to such degradation? Or was there a more macabre side to Taylor's life? The inference arose that he practised witchcraft – at the very least dabbled in it. Could he possibly have found uncanny means whereby to procure famous stars for his private collection of pornography? If the witchcraft theory seems too far fetched, then could there have been another evil form of intoxication used by Taylor? It was known by a few, and following his death by many, that he had more than a passing interest in drugs.

Narcotics were not new to Hollywood in the Twenties. 'Joy powder' (cocaine) was easily available to the rich and famous of Los Angeles. In 1916 English drug expert Aleister Crowley did a study of drug taking in Hollywood. He referred to many of the film folk as 'the cinema crowd of cocaine-crazed, sexual lunatics'. It was only in 1920 that the sale of opium across the counter was outlawed by Prohibition, and by that time many of Hollywood's finest stars were junkies. It became common practice for studios to pep up their money-spinning stars with pills and injections to keep them from dying of exhaustion from making film after film. Many of them, though, died because of drugs, including Wallace Read, Barbara La Marr, Olive Thomas and Alma Rubens.

Taylor had no difficulty in obtaining drugs, even during Prohibition. However, no narcotics were found in Taylor's bungalow following his murder. But then, Charles Eyton and Adolph Zukor had been cleaning Taylor's house for some time before the police arrived.

Could Taylor have supplied his lady friends with suitable 'fixes' before undraping them and himself for the camera? It was, after all, later revealed that he was helping the drugs squad to bust some of Hollywood's pushers. Or were these women of the silver screen really just intoxicated enough by Taylor himself that they would risk their careers just to be a part of his collection of dirty pictures?

And this was the man who 'listened with amazement to the charges of these ministers that we are debauching the morals of the youth of this city'.

No wonder Adolph Zukor and Charles Eyton were so desperate to beat the cops to Taylor's bungalow. The question remains: just what else was there that Zukor managed to destroy that would have revealed the real William Desmond Taylor?

It was a typical Hollywood funeral. As yet not all the truth had come out about William Desmond Taylor, and there was a huge crowd to view the gaudy and extravagant funeral. One by one the procession of famous mourners passed by the open bier to pay their last respects.

Mary Miles Minter was openly distraught and supported by Mrs Shelby. As she came to the bier, she bent down to kiss Taylor's corpse on the lips. She stepped back and said, 'He whispered something to me. It sounded like "I shall always love you, Mary." ' Not surprisingly, there was a tremendous stirring among those who heard this staggering pronouncement.

Within six weeks of Taylor's death, over three hundred men and women confessed to his murder. But by that time, although no one had been charged, the police had built up quite a list of likely suspects, and there was a theory to go with each name.

For a time the police leaned towards the theory that he had been 'silenced' for giving the drugs squad information on drug trafficking. Two names were prominent in the minds of detectives: 'Harry the Chink' and 'Wong Wong Lee'.

Henry Peavey was also under suspicion. It was he who had discovered Taylor's body on the morning of 2 February. Why did he not call the police? He had certainly made quite a show of his grief over the death of his master: if he had killed Taylor, wouldn't such a public display be the perfect way to throw the police off his trail? Who could suspect such a devoted butler?

Mrs MacLean had seen the killer and said, 'It walked like a woman - quick little steps.' Peavey was effeminate with a soprano voice and a mincing walk. He'd had the night off when Taylor was killed; he knew his master would be alone. Had Peavey set up an alibi for himself by actually being elsewhere during that night?

Whoever it was who killed Taylor must have known that he would be alone; that he would probably be spending time in his study; that the butler had the night off. Whoever it was probably knew Taylor well. If it wasn't Peavey, it could well have been the elusive Mr Edward F. Sands, the sacked valet, or so the police felt. The problem was that Sands seemed to have disappeared off the face of the earth. This intensified the suspicions of the police.

Sands's vanishing trick suddenly seemed to reveal a peculiar pattern that surrounded Taylor's life. His brother, Denis, had followed closely in Taylor's footsteps, it turned out. Like Taylor, Denis had also abandoned his family and disappeared without trace. Some time after, Edward F. Sands began serving Taylor as his valet. Sands now seemed like a man with no past as the police explored the possibility that he might have committed the murder. It seemed that as Denis Deane-Tanner left this world, Edward F. Sands entered it.

The police also discovered that Denis Deane-Tanner was wanted for larceny. His disappearance probably had to do with the fact that the police were closing in on him.

Was it just coincidence that Taylor had fired Sands for forging and stealing? And since Taylor knew that Sands was a crook, why did he not inform the police?

Indeed, the question that burned in the minds of the police was, were Denis Deane-Tanner and Edward F. Sands the same man? And if so, could he have killed his older brother after a falling out, to ensure that Taylor never gave him away? Or was Sands simply out for revenge for being fired?

Detectives concluded ultimately that Sands and Denis were indeed one and the same, his dark hair bleached for disguise and his crude manner coached by Taylor into humble impeccability. The police wanted desperately to question him, but he was gone like a wisp of smoke.

Among the ever-growing collection of suspects, the names that top-billed this real-life murder mystery were Mary Miles Minter and Mabel Normand.

Mabel Ethelreid Normand was born on 16 November 1894, the youngest of three children, to Claude G. Normand and Mary Drury. Her place of birth seems to vary between Boston and Rhode Island.

Mother was an Irish Catholic. Father was a Frenchman who played piano in pit orchestras in small theatres, which kept the family on the move. Being born in the trunk, Mabel had very little formal education, but she was a bright girl who could read exceptionally well, and excelled in athletics. By the time she was thirteen and living in New York, she had developed into a very beautiful young creature, and modelled for artists and photographers. She was a born exhibitionist.

At the age of sixteen, and at the prompting of fellow model-cum-actress Alice Joyce, she tried her luck in the movies and managed to get a little acting work at Biograph. She was billed as Muriel Fortesque for a time, but by 1911 she was again Mabel Normand. Aged just seventeen, Mabel fell in love with Biograph actor and director Mack Sennett, some fourteen years her senior. When he left Biograph to form Keystone, she went with him, and he began to turn out the finest series of two-reel comedies of the early Silents. And much of that was due to Mabel.

She was a brilliant actress and a fine comedienne. She hadn't fully developed her talents by the time she left Keystone several years later, but she came to be known ultimately as the 'female Chaplin', which may have aptly described her stature in the industry, but underestimated her own individual genius.

She was Sennett's first major star, and her extrovert nature allowed Sennett to get away with some outrageous pranks. For instance, when Sennett, Mabel and actor-director Henry Lehrman first arrived in Los Angeles in 1912, they stepped off the train into a massive army parade. Sennett had Lehrman go and buy a doll and shawl and sent Mabel, adorned by the shawl and clutching her 'baby', into the crowd. Lehrman turned his camera as Mabel moved along with the marching soldiers, searching for her 'lover'. The reactions she got from the soldiers, who had no idea she was acting, were incredible.

Then one soldier stepped out of his line to help her in her search, upon which Sennett sent his male star, Ford Sterling, on to the scene to engage the soldier in a fight. All hell broke loose as the police leapt in. Mabel and Ford hightailed it down the street with the cops in pursuit. And all the time Lehrman's camera was turning. The Keystone Kops were born!

Mabel was liked by all who knew her, but she was not the sweet innocent teenager the public thought her to be. She lived openly with Sennett in a bizarre relationship. Sennett had just the kind of eccentricity to complement Mabel's own exhibitionist streak. He could, and often did, hit a spittoon at thirty paces with his tobacco juice. He had a huge bath installed in his office in which he soaked for hours at a time; if someone wanted a meeting with him, he'd invite them into his bath.

Mabel's own oddball behaviour was typified by the time she once cartwheeled across a field before a film crew, revealing that she was not wearing any underwear!

Her erratic behaviour was at least consistent during her years with Sennett, but in later years she would become a wild, unpredictable woman while simultaneously realizing her movie potential more fully.

When she was still with Sennett, she began to direct her own pictures. But the young comedian who had only just joined Sennett, Charles Chaplin, was unhappy at having to take direction from her in her own vehicle, *Mabel at the Wheel*. He stopped working midway through a scene and refused to continue until Sennett himself came on to the set and supervised the rest of production. Despite this bust up, Mabel and Chaplin remained good friends while they worked together. It was partly through her efforts and talent that he grew to become the most beloved comic of the silent era, although there are some who still maintain that Mabel Normand was the most brilliant comic of the silent screen.

Chaplin was, under the Tramp's make-up, a handsome fellow, and he had many women in his life. It seems that he would have liked Mabel to have been one of them, for on one occasion he kissed her, to which she gently responded by reminding him that they both owed their loyalties to Sennett. She was, at that time, a one-guy girl.

But in 1915, shortly before Mabel and Mack were due to be married, she discovered him in bed with a friend of hers, Mae Busch, whom she had personally brought from New York to be in movies. Mabel burst in on them and Mae picked up a vase and smashed it over Mabel's head. With blood pouring from her wound, Mabel staggered outside and was found an hour later by the Arbuckles on their porch.

She was never again quite the same. An emotional wound, deeper than the scar that her dark hair thereafter kept secret, stayed with her throughout the rest of her life. Its immediate effect was to lead Mabel to make an attempt on her life. She leapt into the ocean from a pier and was dragged half-dead from the waves. The Arbuckles took her home and tended to her.

She continued to work for Sennett, but their love affair was not to be rekindled. A new phase in her working life began with the formation of the Mabel Normand Feature Film Company, set up by Mack Sennett to allow her the opportunity to make feature-length films and realize her potential as a film-maker.

She made *Mickey*, giving a warm and moving performance as a country tomboy enjoying adventures in the big city. She had proved that she could combine comedy with pathos, but Sennett withheld the release of *Mickey* for two years. It was a huge success, but by then Mabel had signed with Samuel Goldwyn. Goldwyn fell in love with Mabel and she took advantage of it. During the making of one film she suddenly disappeared and weeks later turned up in Paris, spending money like it was going out of style.

During the voyage back, an admiring male passenger made a pass at her, which resulted in her expressing her outrage and demanding a public apology. Before the Captain, the crew and many of the passengers, the man stammered his apology, upon which Mabel said, 'I should think so too. I don't know what made you think I was that kind of a girl,' and she promptly stepped out of her dress and dived naked into the ship's swimming pool.

When they docked in New York, they were met by some of Mabel's friends who persuaded her with little effort to take them on a cruise to France. She immediately booked passage for them and herself, and made the voyage back to France. Goldwyn tolerated this behaviour because of his infatuation for her.

Weeks later, on her return to New York, she was greeted by another group of greedy friends who told her, 'Now it's our turn.' She again booked them and herself passage and was gone for a further couple of months, and still Goldwyn waited to finish his picture. Finally Mabel came home, by which time she had spent half a million dollars.

She became notorious for her wild all-night parties, and rumours spread that she was on drugs. It was a sad fact that she had become addicted to cocaine. She was introduced to drugs by a quiet, gentlemanly actor from the Sennett lot known to his punters simply as 'The Count'. He was always on the lookout for actors who needed something to pick them up or calm them down. The first fix was always free. He started Wallace Reid on the road to oblivion. His other customers included Barbara La Marr, Juanita Hansen and Alma Rubens.

Mabel spent around $2,000 a week on her addiction, which included keeping a blackmailer at bay. William Desmond Taylor, sympathetic to her need for drugs, on one occasion confronted the blackmailer and floored him. By 1922 Mabel was involved with Taylor, willingly responding to his invitation to share his bed and his drugs. She had become a most pathetic creature, and yet her beauty and talent were still evident.

When the dope angle to Taylor's death became public, so too did the revelation that Mabel was a junkie – no wonder she had not wanted to be implicated in any way with Taylor's vices. If she had found her letters to Taylor before the police had, she might have been saved from having the muck raked about her.

Or was her attempt to hide her relationship with Taylor more than just a cover-up for their shared vices? Did she in fact hope to stay out of the investigation altogether? She had been the last to see him alive, and ten minutes after that he had been killed. She had also paid several visits to Roscoe Arbuckle, out on bail for his second trial, and police found that fact plus the fact that she had been the last known person to see Taylor as 'highly significant'. But can the two facts have any connection by any stretch of the imagination?

The truth was that she was a loyal friend to Arbuckle who had aided her in her time of need, and now she supported him when many others in Hollywood turned their backs on him. But at that time Arbuckle had not been acquitted, Taylor's murderer had not been found, and the police tried to put two and two together and lost count.

Was Mabel capable of killing Taylor? And what would her motive have been? The police seemed to have a hard time answering those two questions with any credibility, but still she was a star suspect.

Only one other person shared top billing with her in the Taylor murder case – Mary Miles Minter.

Her real name was Juliet Shelby, and her mother, Charlotte Shelby, was a veritable stage mother. She wanted her little girl to be a big star. Juliet was born on 1 April 1902 and with her mother behind her she quickly became one of the most popular child stars of the American theatre. They knew her as 'Little Juliet Shelby', and by the age of ten she was making motion pictures.

In 1915 Metro Pictures was formed with Richard Rowland as president and Louis B. Mayer as secretary. Olga Petrova was their first big star. They also signed Ethel and Lionel Barrymore, Francis X. Bushman and Juliet Shelby. Juliet now had her name changed to Mary Miles Minter, and Metro groomed her as the natural successor to Mary Pickford, complete with soft, long curls.

Two years later she joined Mutual, and at the age of seventeen was one of their biggest stars. Then in 1919 Adolph Zukor added a new concern, Realart Pictures Corp, to his ever-growing enterprise. He was the most powerful man in Hollywood and commanded the biggest array of movie stars. To his acting stable he added Mary Miles Minter, who was signed up by Realart, and one of her first pictures for Zukor was *Anne of Green Gables*, directed by William Desmond Taylor.

Up to that time it's doubtful that sweet innocent Mary had ever had a boyfriend. Her contract forbade her to desecrate her demure image by getting married or becoming pregnant. Mrs Charlotte Shelby had no intentions of allowing anything to stand in the way of her daughter's career, and any man hoping to possess the young, pretty and highly desirable Mary would do so only over mother's dead body.

But Mary fell hopelessly in love with Taylor, and with or without mother's consent he and Mary had a long affair which, when made public, resulted in the abrupt end of her career. Could Mrs Shelby have known what was going on, bearing in mind that Mary's whole career hung not so much upon her talent as upon her image?

The inference has been drawn that Mrs Shelby had not objected to Mary's involvement with Taylor because she too was receiving sexual favours from him. If it was true, then Taylor was carrying on with four women at the same time. If false, he still had three woman to keep his peculiar lusts satisfied. And any woman involved could have been madly jealous; perhaps jealous enough to kill him.

Zelda Crosby was dead, so she could not answer for herself,

but she had shown by her actions that she was distraught over Taylor's death. The police knew, though, that it was quite common for people to kill themselves after killing a lover.

As for Mabel, she was hardly the jealous type. But she was eccentric, erratic and so hopelessly addicted to cocaine that she might have been crazy enough to do anything.

Mary was something else: she was young and impressionable, and it seemed that she might well have wanted Taylor all for herself. Even at the funeral, she insisted that Taylor, in death, had declared his love for her. Had she wanted to possess him in life and in death?

The police, although high on the Denis Deane-Tanner/ Edward F. Sands theory, could not rule out the fact that Mrs MacLean had said that the figure she saw leaving Taylor's apartment right after the shooting 'walked like a woman – quick little steps and broad hips and short legs'. Mary was certainly broad in the hips, having grown even chubbier by 1922. But then, Mrs Shelby herself was broad in the hips. And she had been seen, as police discovered, practising with her .38-calibre pearl-handled revolver shortly before the murder.

Had Mrs Shelby perhaps killed Taylor in a fit of jealousy? Or was she out to put a bullet in the man who stole her daughter's virtue and so threatened her career?

The William Desmond Taylor murder case had all the best ingredients for a first-class fictional thriller, and yet it was completely true. It could almost have been anybody whodunit.

It could have been Mabel Normand; having left Taylor's apartment (could she count on Mrs MacLean's spying to prove that she left before the killing?), she returned ten minutes later in men's clothing (but curiously forgetful about the letters that would incriminate her).

It could have been Mary Miles Minter: besotted with the man who was twenty-five years her senior and unable to accept sharing him any longer, she killed him and returned, not to her own house, but to her mother's where she knew she would find protection.

It could have been Charlotte Shelby; as possessive as her

daughter, she preferred not to have him at all, rather than share him. Or had she only recently discovered her daughter's affair with Taylor, and then taken drastic steps to end the relationship in the hope of saving Mary's career?

It could have been Zelda Crosby; insanely jealous, she killed the man she loved and, unable to live without him, took her own life.

It could have been Edward F. Sands (or should that be Denis Deane-Tanner?); bent on revenge or determined to silence Taylor permanently, he returned to the bungalow on Peavey's night off and pumped two bullets into his former employer's (brother's?) back.

It could have been Henry Peavey, his devotion to his 'massa' spilling over into homosexual passion but unable to overcome Taylor's obsession with women, he returned on his night off for a single moment – long enough to fire two shots.

It could have been 'Harry the Chink' or 'Wong Wong Lee'; or it could have been just about anybody else who allowed themselves to get mixed up with Taylor's perverse activities.

It was truly a bizarre case. But more bizarre than anything so far mentioned was the fact that no charges were ever brought against anyone for the murder of Taylor. Suddenly the case was closed and classified as 'unsolved'.

Was it that the police were really unable to unravel the mystery? Or was there a cover-up?

It was following the murder of Taylor, and while Arbuckle was still standing trial for manslaughter, that Adolph Zukor headed a conglomerate of Hollywood's movie moguls – Marcus Loew, Carl Laemmle, Samuel Goldwyn, William Fox, Lewis and Myron Selznick – who elected postmaster general William H. Hays as president of the newly-formed Motion Picture Producers and Distributors of America Inc. – the official Hollywood watchdog.

Its prime function was to purify Hollywood with a vengeance. Censorship was introduced, and movie stars, no matter how beloved by the public, who threatened any hint of a scandal were immediately blacklisted. Hays had his notorious 'doom book' compiled, using spies in all quarters of Hollywood life to weed out the undesirable.

It was in all a frantic effort to prevent anything like the Arbuckle and Taylor scandals ever happening again. The Arbuckle case was still in court with acquittal for Roscoe some time in the future and his career already terminated by Will Hays. Taylor was dead and a number of famous names implicated in the worst way, and the outcome of this case could prove disastrous for Paramount and the rest of the industry. But most of all for Zukor.

The careers of a number of people may have already been ruined – both Mabel Mormand and Mary Miles Minter were having their pictures withdrawn from cinemas – but was it possible for a man like Zukor, the most powerful of all the studio heads, to ensure that it didn't go any further?

You will recall how the police first arrived at Taylor's bungalow to discover a number of characters involved in highly dubious activities. Among them were Zukor and Charles Eyton. Doesn't it seem odd that these two men seemed to escape being questioned at length and ultimately implicated in any way? Why would the police have allowed two such witnesses found at the scene of the crime destroying potential evidence to pass virtually unnoticed in the affair?

Was it for the same reason that no one was ever charged with Taylor's murder?

According to King Vidor, a top director from that era, it was a complete Hollywood cover-up, probably organized by Will Hays, the official Hollywood watchdog, who bribed the police to drop the case.

The cover-up was certainly complete. The murderer was never brought to justice. However, Hollywood and Will Hays had their own means of meting out justice, and not necessarily to the innocent.

Mabel's career was all but over; her current release, *Suzanna*, was boycotted and eventually withdrawn. The public made it clear they no longer wanted her. She went on to make several two-reelers for Hal Roach, fading gently rather than abruptly disappearing.

It is possible that, because of her unique talent, she may have made a comeback at some time, if it hadn't been for a further scandal in 1924.

On New York's Day she arrived at the apartment of an oil magnate, Cortland S. Dines, where he was entertaining Edna Purviance. Both Edna and Dines had been drinking heavily and were in a state of undress. Exactly what happened next is not certain, because of the vagueness of all concerned. When Mabel's chauffeur arrived to collect her, he somehow crossed words with Dines and brought the argument to an abrupt end by pulling a revolver, which belonged to Mabel, and shooting Dines.

Dines survived the shooting. A hearing was called, but neither he nor any of the others clarified exactly what happened. Dines said he was drunk and could recall nothing of the matter.

The image of Edna and Mabel cavorting with Dines and then the chauffeur shooting the oil tycoon was more than enough, coming so close on the heels of the Taylor scandal, to bring Mabel's film career to an end. She did have one last completed film in the can, but it was never released.

In a futile effort to save some semblance of her life, she married actor Lew Cody. But whatever happiness they had was short-lived. Mabel died of pneumonia and tuberculosis in 1930, although her death could be more accurately attributed to drugs. Four years later, Cody's heart failed him.

Mary Miles Minter made no attempt to resuscitate her career. She retired involuntarily from the screen almost at the moment when her involvement with Taylor was made known. But for her the sordid affair didn't end there.

Fifteen years later a woman claiming to be Mrs Ada Deane-Tanner, the wife of Denis Deane-Tanner, appeared before the Los Angeles District Attorney in a peculiar attempt to clear her husband's name in the Taylor case. In the process she succeeded in casting further suspicion upon Mary Miles Minter who attended the hearing with her mother. Mary was now a sorry sight, her mere thirty-five years hanging heavy on her with obesity.

In court, listening to the case gradually being turned against her, she stood up and cried, 'Try me for the murder of William Desmond Taylor, or declare that you have no evidence against me.'

No evidence was forthcoming. No charge was made. Mary was free to live out the rest of her days in seclusion in Santa Monica, refusing to talk to anyone about the scandal or her involvement with Taylor, except to insist that a great deal had been made out of nothing.

To this day, Hollywood's first murder mystery remains unsolved. However, it was always said by those around at the time that the identity of the murderer was an open secret in Hollywood. It was, they said, Mrs Charlotte Shelby. According to an unwritten law of those days, a mother or father had every right to kill a man who took a daughter's virginity outside of marriage. But the fact was, for whatever reason, that the police didn't charge Mrs Shelby, or anyone else, and the so-called 'open secret' remains pure supposition.

And so the case remains unsolved, although what is almost certain is that the name of the killer is to be found somewhere in these pages; the question still hangs over Hollywood's most famous murder mystery – who really did it?

CASE 2

Thomas Ince: M-m-m-m-Murder?

IN NOVEMBER 1924 Thomas Harper Ince, a pioneer of the cinema and one of the most important and influential figures in the history of American motion pictures, died. Exactly how and where has, since 1924, been a subject of much conjecture. The reason for this is the abundance of contradicting evidence and the unabashed falsehoods that immediately followed Ince's death.

There are a few who insist that there was no mystery to the death; that the official verdict, which was death from natural causes, says it all. But does it?

There are basically two accounts of Ince's death; only one of them can be true. If the 'official' account can be found to be in harmony with the evidence and testimonies that preceded it, then much fuss has been made about nothing for the past six decades.

But what if the official version fails to match the evidence? Do we then have a clear-cut case of murder and corruption? We start with the unofficial version which includes certain elements which Hearst always hotly denied.

William Randolph Hearst was distraught at reading in *The New York Daily Times* that Charles Chaplin was continuing to pay 'ardent attention' to Marion Davies in Hollywood. The newspaper went on to report that Chaplin had dined and danced with Marion at Montmartre's night spot. When a lovely young dancer entertained that evening, Chaplin applauded loudly, but he never once took his eyes off the beautiful, blonde Marion.

Hearst was hurt, angry and resentful. He had made Marion what she was today; he had given her everything except a wedding ring because his wife refused to consent to a divorce under any circumstances. Hearst may have been a man of power, but even he couldn't divorce his wife and marry Marion

whom he adored more than anything. Even more than money –
and money was something he didn't lack for.

He had created a newspaper empire that, in his own way, gave
him more power than even the President of the United States.
Virtually single-handedly he used his newspapers to force
America into the Spanish-American War – and boosted circula-
tion figures. Through his newspapers he helped to put both
Theodore and Franklin Delano Roosevelt in the White House.

He could elevate anyone to a state of near royalty if they
found favour with him; anyone who fell from grace with him
could expect to find their names raked through the slime in the
pages of Hearst's papers. Hearst had been instrumental in
turning public opinion against Arbuckle in the early months of
that particular scandal. Hearst was not shy of fabrication when
he thought it necessary. As well as being a ferocious enemy, he
was also very loyal to those he esteemed as friends, and being a
multi-millionaire he chose his friends very carefully.

At one stage, he had no more than a passing interest in
movies, and his newspapers did not devote a great deal of space
to motion pictures or movie stars, but in 1917 he met a
struggling young blonde starlet, Marion Davies. He was then
fifty-four and married. She was just twenty, very beautiful and
inclined to stammer. She had made just one film, *Runaway
Romany*, but although she fared well in this Mary Pickford-type
vehicle, it was clear that she was not a great actress.

Hearst was smitten with her and promised her that he would
personally turn her into the greatest ever movie star. He had her
privately tutored by a drama teacher and successfully arranged
for her first starring role in *Cecilia of the Pink Roses* in 1918. By
direct orders of Hearst, his newspapers positively went overboard in their praise for the film and its new star:

'A movie masterpiece.'

'Marion Davies . . . a vision of loveliness.'

'A bewitching beauty.'

Other newspapers were decidedly less enthusiastic.

Marion began living openly with Hearst, and they main-
tained several homes, including their famous San Simeon castle.
But any mention of their affair was kept out of the press.
However, not a day went by when her name didn't appear in his

newspapers, lauding her glory. He was turning her into a star simply through publicity.

In 1919 Hearst made an agreement with Adolph Zukor to release her pictures through Paramount. To make Marion Davies pictures, Hearst set up Cosmopolitan, and he ploughed thousands of dollars into her movies, which were usually lavish historical spectaculars. They were so costly that they all lost money. Nevertheless, Hearst continued to repeat the formula, and in 1922 he produced *When Knighthood Was in Flower* at the staggering cost of one-and-a-half-million dollars. It actually turned a profit, and Hearst's newspapers praised it to the skies:

'Marion Davies soars to new heights.'

'Superlative performance by the talented star.'

But despite his own enthusiasm for Marion and her pictures, over the years Hearst lost seven million dollars producing her films. But then his entire fortune ran to some four hundred million dollars, and he felt his money was well spent.

He allowed her to spend as much as she wanted. She threw extravagant beach parties at her 'Beach House' which surpassed anything that even Hollywood had seen before. At one such party, in 1922, following her return from a European trip, a guest, high on bootleg whisky, was hurt in a shooting incident. The police arrived, reporters got hold of the story, and it appeared in the newspapers the next day. But not in Hearst's newspapers. In fact, he had Marion's lawyers phone all of the other newspapers to insist that she was not even at the party, even though Hearst had thrown it in her honour.

In 1924 Cosmopolitan moved over to the Goldwyn company, and Hearst made plans to have Marion's films, which were all previously shot in New York, made in California. In an effort to find a base on the West Coast, Hearst was negotiating with Tom Ince to use his Culver City studio. But when *The New York Daily Times* reported Marion's night out on the town in Los Angeles with Chaplin, Hearst was far away in New York.

It was not, however, a revelation to Hearst that Chaplin and Davies were meeting. He had kept tabs on Marion's association with Chaplin and had hired private detectives to watch her when Hearst was away. One day he even rang her and read out a detective's report of her involvement with Chaplin, but she insisted that they were purely friends. Hearst, although jealous, took no serious steps to end Marion's relationship with Chaplin. He loved her too much to jeopardize their own affair, and he had great admiration for Charlie Chaplin. But it galled him to know that they were carrying on behind his back, and he decided to return immediately to California.

Chaplin's hair was grey, and he wore no moustache. He was thirty-five, not very tall, and very handsome. He was the most successful all-round film-maker in the world. He wrote, produced, directed and starred in his own pictures, and in each of his activities his genius shone through.

But his private life was a mess, and Marion helped to make life a little more bearable. Many of his domestic problems were of his own making. Somehow he could not direct his own love life as well as he could direct a feature-length comedy such as *The Gold Rush*.

The making of that particular film had begun happily, but his obsession with the young female lead of the film, Lita Grey, aged sixteen, led to personal disaster. Lita (real name Lillita McMurray) had done a number of walk-on parts in some of Chaplin's films; now she had blossomed into a beautiful young teenager, and he felt she was perfect for the lead female role in *The Gold Rush*.

But as filming progressed he began to feel that she was all wrong for the part after all. She just didn't seem to photograph well, and he exposed miles of film of her in the dancehall sequence, trying to capture the magic he was looking for. For days she danced in front of the camera, the klieg lights belting down on her as she tried to satisfy her director. Suddenly she stopped dancing, grabbed hold of her stomach and screamed in agony. Chaplin rushed over to her, and looking up at him she announced faintly that she was pregnant. Chaplin was the father.

He should have known better. Eight years earlier he had been foolish enough to get involved with a fourteen-year-old girl, Mildred Harris. When she was sixteen she had told Chaplin that she was pregnant, and Charlie suddenly saw the headlines forming in his mind: CHAPLIN ON STATUTORY RAPE CHARGE.

He married Mildred, and she gave birth. The child was tragically deformed, and died three days later.

It was a disastrous marriage from the very beginning. Charlie mourned his dead son, but Mildred played around. She would leave his bed at night to share one with Russian actress Alla Nazimova. Life became intolerable for Charlie. She accused him of cruelty; he accused her of infidelity. The inevitable result was divorce, and the muck flew think and fast in court and in the tabloids. But Chaplin, in some peculiar loyal way, never revealed that Mildred's lover was the famous lesbian actress from Russia.

Now he found himself facing a shotgun wedding again, only this time he didn't want any kind of a wedding. But on to the scene came Lita's Uncle Edwin McMurray, a lawyer, warning Charlie that he was guilty of statutory rape. Chaplin offered Lita a dowry of $20,000 as well as all the help she needed to find a suitable husband. But Uncle Ed had other ideas. He wanted his niece to marry Chaplin, as did Lita's mother who stood hungrily by.

So Charlie took solace in the arms of Marion Davies. They met secretly, usually at Chaplin's home. He was still busily engaged in making *The Gold Rush* and she was at the Goldwyn studio filming *Zander the Great*. They took every opportunity to get together, daring only occasionally to go out in public together. One such time was at Montmartre's, where the reporter from *The New York Daily Times* noticed how Chaplin seemed in awe of his blonde companion, and duly reported it.

A day later Charlie received an invitation from William Randolph Hearst to join him and a number of other guests, including Marion, on board his 280-foot yacht, *Oneida*, for a fun-filled cruise to San Diego and Baja.

The same invitation arrived at the home of Thomas Ince. It would be, Hearst had felt, a good opportunity to celebrate Ince's forty-first birthday, which had taken place on 6 November. Ince accepted the invitation, but said he wouldn't be able to make it until the day after the *Ondeia* set sail because he had the premiere of *The Mirage* to attend. He told Hearst that he would meet them the following day at San Diego for the big party Hearst said that he would throw in honour in Ince.

Like many of his peers, Tom Ince had begun his working life as an actor. He considered himself a serious stage actor and only consented to appear in films when he was otherwise out of work. In 1910, with no prospect of any future stage work, he began appearing regularly in Biograph pictures, and then joined Carl Laemmle's IMP where he directed a number of Mary Pickford's films, many of which were shot in Cuba to escape the dirty deeds of the Motion Picture Patents Company.

In 1911 he left IMP and went to work in Los Angeles for the New York Motion Pictures company, making a successful series of westerns. The quality of his pictures was outstanding. He had an eye for fine detail, and he wrote most of the tightly structured scripts himself. He even retained a Wild West Show and used them to great effect in many spectacular horse operas.

As his reputation and stature grew, he purchased 20,000 acres of land and built his own studio, which he called Inceville. He was now writing and producing so many pictures that he had to give up directing all of them, leaving many of his westerns in the hands of Francis Ford, John Ford's brother.

In 1915, Ince was working side by side with the legendary D.W. Griffith in the new Triangle Film Corporation. In 1916 Ince produced his most famous picture, *Civilization*, which vied for attention and acclaim with Griffith's *Intolerance*. He directed some of it, but left a great many scenes to some of his other directors.

In 1918 he left Triangle, formed his own company, and built new studios at Culver City. He enjoyed great success as an independent producer, but never considered himself a movie mogul. In 1920, Louis Delluc, the French devotee of movies, wrote: 'Griffith is cinema's first director. Ince is its first prophet.'

He might well have continued his reign as an independent film-maker well into the Talkies, but instead he accepted Hearst's invitation.

Louella Parsons was a journalist from New York, in Hollywood at the invitation of Hearst, and ready for her first taste of Hollywood gossip on board the *Oneida*. She was thirty-one and not yet the aged battleaxe who walked over whomever she liked

The career of Mary Miles Minter, one of Hollywood's leading child performers and, later, romantic leads, never recovered from the blow dealt it by the murder in 1922 of her reputed lover, William Desmond Taylor, seen here on the right of the picture; on the left is Alan Connor.

Mabel Normand was also romantically linked with Taylor, and the police found the fact that she was the last known person to see him 'highly significant'.

The inability of two juries to agree led to comedian Roscoe 'Fatty' Arbuckle (second from right) being tried three times for the murder of Virginia Rappe, who died in 1921 following one of his parties.

Thomas Harper Ince, one of the most important and influential figures in the history of American motion pictures, died in November 1924. Was he shot in mistake for Charlie Chaplin?

Marion Davies, protegee of newspaper magnate William Randolph Hearst, was renowned for her parties attended by stars such as Leslie Howard (in the pierrot costume) and Ramon Navarro (as the Indian prince). She was rumoured to be carrying on an affair with Chaplin at the time of the death of Thomas Ince.

(or rather didn't like) in what became her ridiculously influential column.

She was at the studio with Marion Davies when Charlie Chaplin came to pick them both up in his chauffeur-driven car. At the wheel was Charlie's faithful driver and friend, Japanese-born Toriachi Kono. Vera Burnett, Marion's stand-in on *Zander the Great*, stood and watched enviously as the trio set off for what promised to be a memorable weekend.

The excited guests boarded the *Oneida* at San Pedro. Among them were actresses Margaret Livingston, Aileen Pringle, Seena Owen and Julanna Johnston, Marion's sisters Ethel and Reine, writer Elinor Glyn, Hearst's production head Dr Daniel Carson Goodman, Hearst's secretary Joseph Willcombe and Ince's business manager George H. Thomas.

A stock of vintage champagne was stowed away, and a jazz band happily press-ganged. There was food in plenty. A good time was had by all. The *Oneida* sailed a southern route, passing Catalina and heading down towards San Diego and Baja. Hearst moored at San Diego to await the arrival of Tom Ince.

The following day, Sunday, Ince arrived, and Marion welcomed him aboard by signalling naval-style with a huge bunch of balloons in each hand. Despite the cases of illegal booze on board, Ince abstained. He suffered from a pre-ulcerated stomach, and his doctor had warned him more than once about eating and drinking in excess. He spent much of the time discussing details of the plans to shoot Marion's pictures at his studio.

There are two theories about what happened next. One is that during the party Hearst became acutely aware that both Marion and Charlie were missing. He went in search of them and discovered them, on a lower deck, with Chaplin writhing passionately on top of Marion. Suddenly she saw her elderly and insanely jealous lover standing over them, and let out a stammered scream.

'M-m-m-murder!'

Guests came running in time to see Hearst aiming a pistol at Chaplin. Confusion suddenly reigned, and the gun fired. A man dropped to the deck. It was not Chaplin. It was Tom Ince.

The other version, which has been strongly rumoured, was

that during the party Hearst missed Marion, and went in search of her. He discovered her on a lower galley sitting at a table talking to a man whose back was to Hearst. The hair was grey and curly. Hearst knew it had to be Chaplin. Seeing them together he was suddenly crazed with jealousy. He raced to his cabin and took the diamond-studded revolver he kept on board to shoot down seagulls.

He came up behind the man, the gun pointing to his head. Marion screamed in horror.

'M-m-m-murder!'

Hearst fired. The man dropped to the floor. It was not Chaplin, but Thomas Ince.

The following day Toriachi Kono was summoned by Chaplin to San Diego. Charlie felt it best to leave the yacht, and while Kono waited for him, Ince was carried unconscious from the yacht. Kono was horrified by what he saw. There was a bullet hole in Ince's head. Dr Daniel Carson Goodman went with Ince and, probably the next day, Ince died in a hotel room in Del Mar.

Meanwhile, Hearst had gathered the shell-shocked guests about him and 'convinced' each and every one of them that the wisest course was to say nothing about the events aboard the *Oneida*. Some even felt it safer to insist that they had not been there. Louella Parsons headed back to New York with a promise from Hearst that she would thereafter syndicate her column through his newspapers, ultimately making her one of the most powerful figures in movie history with just a gossip column.

Ince's funeral was held in Hollywood on 21 November. His wife Nell was accompanied by her two sons and Tom's brothers, Ralph and John. Marion was also there but, conspicuously, Hearst was not. Douglas Fairbanks and Mary Pickford paid their last respects. So too did Harold Lloyd.

Charlie was also at the funeral. Two days later, on the Sunday, he was on his way south by train to marry Lita Grey in Mexico. His affair with Marion was suddenly over, and another disastrous marriage ensued, ending in Chaplin's most degrading and disturbing divorce case almost three years later. In his desperation to escape the seemingly inevitable scandal over Ince's death, Chaplin had leapt straight out of the frying pan into the fire.

Ince was cremated without an inquest, with only those on board the *Oneida* knowing exactly how Tom Ince, 'The Father of the Western' and the cinema's 'first prophet', died.

We now go back to before the death of Thomas Ince, to recreate the 'official' version as accepted by San Diego's District Attorney, Chester Kemply.

Events prior to the Saturday of 15 November were much the same as in the account just given. Hearst was in New York, suspicious of Marion's relationship with Chaplin. He had read the little story in *The New York Daily Times* of their night out at Montmartre's and he had been receiving information from a private detective about how much time Marion and Charlie were spending together.

But he needn't have worried. It is an old cliché, but Charlie and Marion really were 'just good friends'. She had been a comfort to him through the tribulations he was facing over Lita's pregnancy and the pressure on him from Uncle Ed and Mrs McMurray for him to marry the girl. It was true that Marion was fond of Chaplin – very fond – but there was no affair.

The idea to throw a party on the *Oneida* was in the main to celebrate the birthday of Tom Ince, even if it was a week or so overdue. Hearst and Ince were in the midst of negotiations for all of Marion's films to be shot at his Culver City Studio. But Ince let Hearst know that he would not be able to make the departure from San Pedro because of a premiere he had to attend, but he would meet them at San Diego on the Sunday.

Chaplin had also been invited. Despite his suspicions, Hearst liked Charlie, and besides, the cruise would allow him to see exactly how Chaplin and Marion behaved together. But Charlie declined the invitation because of the pressure of filming *The Gold Rush*. Lita's pregnancy had forced her out of production and she had been replaced by Georgia Hale. Many scenes had to be reshot and Charlie, being a perfectionist to a fault, was willing to spend any amount of time on getting what he wanted. His films took for ever to make, and *The Gold Rush* was no exception.

So the guests, minus Chaplin, boarded the *Oneida* on the Saturday. (Louella Parsons, then an unimportant columnist, was not among the party but still busily typing away in New York.)

The champagne flowed and the guests danced to the sounds of the jazz band. When Ince came aboard the next day at San Diego, he was tired but willing to talk business. He was also, of course, the guest of honour, since it was his birthday they were celebrating. He ate well but didn't drink.

The following morning Dr Goodman and Ince rose early to catch a train back to Los Angeles. The party may not have been officially over, but they at least had work to get on with. But Ince was unwell. He had been awake for much of the night with indigestion. His stomach was pre-ulcerated and he figured he had foolishly overindulged.

Before they reached the station, Ince felt a pain in his chest. Dr Goodman helped him on to the train, but as they pulled into Del Mar, Ince suffered a major heart attack. Dr Goodman got him straight off the train and into the nearest hotel from where he rang Nell Ince, Tom's wife, and told her of her husband's illness. Then he called a doctor and waited for him to arrive before continuing on to Los Angeles. Some time after he left, Ince died. Dr Goodman had diagnosed 'acute indigestion'.

On Wednesday, 19 November, *The Los Angeles Times* announced the death of Tom Ince with the headline: MOVIE PRODUCER SHOT ON HEARST YACHT. Later in the day further editions omitted the story without any explanation.

Then the Hearst newspapers began putting out their version of how Ince died:

> #### SPECIAL CAR RUSHES STRICKEN
> #### MAN HOME FROM RANCH
> Ince, with his wife, Nell, and his two young sons, had been visiting William Randolph Hearst at his upstate ranch for several days previous to the attack.
>
> When the illness came upon him suddenly the film magnate, stricken unconscious, was removed to a

special car attended by two specialists and three nurses, and hurried back to his canyon home.

His wife and sons, and his brothers, Ralph and John, were at his bedside when the end came.

There was not the slightest hint that Ince had ever set foot on the *Oneida*. In fact, the story, without even mentioning the *Oneida*, silently denied that Ince was on board. But the story was a complete fabrication. Witnesses had seen Ince board the yacht at San Diego, and Hearst was unable to deny it. So he changed the story, admitting Ince was on board, but he claimed that he had died from acute indigestion, as diagnosed by Dr Goodman.

However, as rumours rapidly spread that Ince had been shot by Hearst, the newspaper tycoon marshalled all his forces and mustered all his power to deny them. Marion Davies said that Hearst didn't even carry a gun on his yacht. But many who had sailed with him before knew that he did keep a diamond-studded revolver and took delight in shooting down seagulls as part of his guests' entertainment.

In an effort to suppress the rumour, Marion even claimed that Ince had died two days after returning to his home because a member of his family was a Christian Scientist and therefore wouldn't allow a doctor to treat him.

If, as Hearst and his consorts always maintained, Ince died from acute indigestion, why were there so many fabrications? Why was there, in essence, a cover-up?

Perhaps at the crux of the controversy is the question of Chaplin's implication in the whole affair. The 'murder theory' could only ring true if Chaplin were on board the *Oneida* at the time of the shooting. Without Chaplin, Hearst could not have mistaken Ince for the comedian, or indeed, if the other portion of the murder theory is to stand any chance of credibility, Chaplin had to be on board to have been found with Marion by Hearst, sending the newspaper tycoon into a jealous rage.

So if Chaplin was not on board, the 'official' version stands a much better chance of credibility, since without Chaplin there could have been no murder.

All this put poor Charlie into an impossible situation. If he had been on board, and admitted it, he would become implicated in a murder case that centred around his affair with Marion. Chaplin was already in trouble over his affair with Lita Grey, so more of the same kind of scandal would not help him at all. It's also most likely, being the gentleman that he was (remember how he never revealed that Mildred Harris was a lesbian?), that his main concern was for Marion. His admitted presence on the yacht would only mar her image, and he would not have wanted to bring that upon her. Even if he had been on board, then, he would have had to deny it.

What did Chaplin have to say about the affair? In his autobiography very little indeed, except that Ince survived for three weeks after being taken ill and had received visits from Marion, Hearst and Chaplin himself! That in itself hardly harmonizes with even the 'official version', since Ince was cremated on 21 November, only four days after he supposedly fell fatally ill.

Other than that, Chaplin always insisted that he was not on the *Oneida* when Ince was struck down.

Why, then, was his chauffuer, Kono, at San Diego?

Also, how do we account for the fact that Vera Burnett, Marion's stand-in, said that she saw Marion and Charlie at the studio, departing for the yacht at San Pedro?

Which brings us to another mystery; if Louella Parsons was still in New York, as she insisted she was, how did Vera Burnett come to see her also at the studio with Chaplin and Davies?

But perhaps the most devastating piece of testimony given against Hearst and his version of what happened comes from Chaplin's faithful Kono. He told actress Eleanor Boardman that while he was at San Diego, he saw Ince carried off the yacht with a bullet hole in his head. He also told the same story to the whole of Chaplin's Japanese staff.

So how reliable a witness was Toriachi Kono?

He had been engaged as Chaplin's chauffeur by the comedian's personal secretary, Tom Harrington. Kono was just twenty-eight and from a well-off middle-class family in Hiroshima. He had immigrated to the States to avoid a career in the family business after several of his own commercial ventures had failed. He fancied a career as an aviator in America, but his young wife dissuaded him from the course, and so he became a chauffeur and eventually found himself driving for Charlie Chaplin.

Chaplin was so impressed with him that he took to hiring an all-Japanese staff. Kono was efficient and discreet. He was totally loyal to Chaplin, and never said or did anything purposely to compromise him.

In all, Kono was with Chaplin for eighteen years, during which time he took on the trusted roles of special confidant and emissary. Only after he felt his position as Chaplin's home organizer was being usurped by Paulette Goddard in 1933 did he leave Chaplin's employ. Charlie was devastated to see him go, and gave him and his wife a gift of $1,000 each, as well as arranging for Kono to work for United Artists in Tokyo.

This was the man who told numerous people, before he knew exactly what the situation was regarding Chaplin's implication, that he had definitely seen Ince with a bullet hole in his head. Is he a man to be believed?

One of the people he had talked to, Eleanor Boardman, learned later from Elinor Glyn, one of the guests on the *Oneida*, that everyone indeed had been sworn to secrecy. If this was so, then Hearst must have been most persuasive. Many of those on board were in his employ anyway and would not wish to lose their jobs. Others must have met with certain favours. Louella Parsons, for instance, soon after the incident saw her column syndicated exclusively through Hearst's newspapers, thus marking her place in cinematic history as one of the two most influential and powerful Hollywood columnists (the other being Hedda Hopper).

If there had been a cover-up - and Hearst had been busily engaged in ensuring that everyone involved cooperated - then what about that first fabricated story about Ince dying at his home surrounded by his wife, Nell, two sons and two brothers? Is there any way Ince's widow and other bereaved members of the family could be so easily bought?

There is no certain answer to that, but it should be noted that at this time Nell knew that Tom was having an affair with another woman, the actress Margaret Livingston, and that the ever-generous Hearst provided a special trust fund for Nell. How Hearst might have 'bought' the brothers, Ralph and John, both noted film-makers, is open to question and speculation.

It must also be said that Vera Burnett later stopped insisting that she had seen either Chaplin or Parsons picking Marion Davies up at the studio, as she had earlier claimed. She was in Hearst's employ and continued to serve as Marion's stand-in.

Certainly William Randolph Hearst was the kind of man who, if he could elevate Presidents and force his country into wars, could certainly cover up a major crime. *If* there had been a crime.

The defence which Hearst erected against the accusers did not stop the rumours. Finally, San Diego's District Attorney, Chester Kemply, was compelled to hold a hearing on the matter, to ascertain once and for all how Ince had died. Before the hearing, he questioned both the doctor and the nurse who had attended to Ince while at the hotel in Del Mar. Their story bore out Hearst's version. But there were still those who had been on board the *Oneida* to testify. Perhaps under oath some of the witnesses might spill the beans and break their vow of silence, if, that is, Eleanor Boardman had got the story right from Elinor Glyn. This was the last chance for the truth to come out. Ince's body was in ashes, and so an autopsy was out of the question.

Peculiarly, Kemply called only one single witness to testify. It was Dr Daniel Carson Goodman, Hearst's production manager and the man who claimed to have diagnosed 'acute indigestion'.

Said Dr Goodman,

On Saturday November 15th, I took the *Oneida*, which belongs to International Film Corporation, with a party on board, to San Diego. Mr Ince was to have been one of the party. He was unable to leave Saturday, stating that he had to work, but would join us Sunday morning.

When he arrived on board he complained of nothing but being tired. Ince discussed during the day details of his agreement just made with International Film Corporation to produce pictures in combination. Ince seemed well. He ate a hearty dinner, retired early.

Next morning he and I arose early before any of the other guests to return to Los Angeles. Ince complained that during the night he had had an attack of indigestion, and still felt bad.

On the way to the station he complained of a pain in the heart. We boarded the train, but at Del Mar a heart attack came upon him. I thought it best to take him off the train, insist upon his resting in a hotel.

I telephoned Mrs Ince that her husband was not feeling well. I called in a physician and remained myself until the afternoon, when I continued on to Los Angeles.

Mr Ince told me that he had had similar attacks before, but that they had not amounted to anything. Mr Ince gave no evidence of having had any liquor of any kind.

My knowledge as a physician enabled me to diagnose the case as one of acute indigestion.

DA Kemply pondered briefly on Dr Goodman's words, and then said:

I began this investigation because of many rumours brought to my office regarding the case, and have considered them until today in order to definitely dispose of them.

There will be no further investigation of stories of drinking on board the yacht. If there are to be, then they will have to be in Los Angeles County where presumably the liquor was secured. People interested in Ince's sudden death have continued to come to me with persistent reports and in order to satisfy them I did conduct an investigation.

But after questioning the doctor and nurse who attended Mr Ince at Del Mar I am satisfied his death was from ordinary causes.

Incredibly, that was the end of the case. Ince was dead and buried – or cremated. And Hearst hoped, whatever his reasons were, that the whole episode was too. For the rest of his life, no one ever dared mention the name of Tom Ince in his presence.

D.W. Griffith noted: 'All you have to do to make Hearst turn white as a ghost is mention Ince's name. There's plenty wrong there, but Hearst is too big to touch.'

Many spoke out publicly in disgust at the so-called investigation. *The Long Beach News* made a scathing attack on the verdict and on District Attorney Kemply, predicting 'that some day one of the scandal-scented mysteries of filmdom will be cleared up'. It demanded that a full investigation be carried out and that justice be seen to be done. It also asserted that if there was any liquor on board Hearst's yacht – a crime in itself during Prohibition – then that was also a matter for investigation, whether Hearst was a millionaire or not. It then went on to describe DA Kemply, who saw 'no reason' to investigate the death of Ince, as 'the best agent Bolshevists could employ in this country'.

Despite the fuss, the matter was officially dropped. Hearst went on to live to the grand old age of eighty-eight. Marion stuck with him to the end, even helping her millionaire lover when he faced a financial crisis by giving him a million of her own dollars. She proved by that charitable act that she could afford not to work, so in 1937 at the age of forty and a proven failure in Talkies, she retired from the screen. Four months after Hearst's death, she married 'for the first time' as one newspaper cynically noted. She was then fifty-four, fat and very rich.

Nell Ince fared less well. The trust which Hearst set up for her was wiped out in the Great Depression, and she ended up driving cabs.

As to the 'murder' of Tom Ince, it remains a matter of conjecture and speculation. Many, however, refute that he was murdered, such as one or two of the numerous Chaplin biographers, and David Niven in his bestseller *Bring On the Empty Horses*, even though Niven wasn't in Hollywood at that time. He, like many of the others who refute the murder theory, inevitably ridicule the very idea by pushing it far into the realms of fantasy by claiming that the theory was that Hearst had pushed Ince's body overboard and the body was never found. As has been shown, that was not the theory at all.

But there are many others who have written about that time in Hollywood, either in reference books or biographies, who still question the death of Ince. Not everybody is convinced by Hearst's story, and probably never will be, whatever the truth of it.

Only those involved knew for certain what happened, and all of them are dead now. Only the contradictory evidence remains and too many unanswered questions, ensuring that despite the official outcome the death of Thomas Ince remains a mystery that won't be laid to rest.

Almost as though the ghost of Thomas H. Ince can't rest either.

Paul Kelly: Convicted Killer

DOROTHY MACKAYE was no raving beauty – she was cute perhaps, more like the girl next door. At twenty-four she was pleasantly plump, of medium height with a pert face that sported a double chin. Her red hair was matched by a number of prominent freckles, especially around her almost Oriental eyes. A crooked front tooth caused her to lisp. She may not have been everyone's idea of a glamour girl, but there were at least two men who loved her – enough to fight over her at her Hollywood apartment while she was in town buying Easter eggs.

Unaware of the brawl that had taken place, she returned to her apartment on that spring evening of 16 April 1927 to find her place a wreck and her husband, Ray Raymond, prostrate, his face bruised and bloody. It was certainly not a sight that he would have wanted his public to see. At thirty-three, he was a popular song-and-dance man who had made his name in *The Ziegfeld Follies* of 1918 and 1919. It was in 1920, when he starred in *Blue Eyes* on Broadway, that he fell in love with a fellow cast member – Dorothy MacKaye.

Born in Scotland, Dorothy had toured Britain's vaudeville stages by the age of four. As a teenager she tried her hand at drama and scored a huge success in *Peg O' My Heart*, which ran for two years. But it was in comedy and musicals that she found her niche, winding up on Broadway where she fell in love at first sight with Ray Raymond. They were quickly married.

Now, as Dorothy helped him to his feet, he looked a sorry sight on legs that were wobbly not just from the beating, but also from too much booze. She guided him to the bedroom and eased him into bed. Despite his injuries, he was in good humour and made a crack about the fight to their black maid, Ethel Lee, who'd concerned herself during the brawl with trying to save the furniture.

He fell asleep. The next morning he didn't wake up. Two days later he died.

Distressed and panic-stricken, Dorothy called Dr Walter Sullivan, a personal friend who knew that any scandal would destroy her career. He certified that Ray had died from complications caused by past illnesses. The subsequent inquest bore out his diagnosis, finding that Raymond had died of kidney trouble and cerebral haemorrhage, due probably to Ray's acute alcoholism.

And that's how the verdict would have remained if police hadn't talked to Ethel Lee who revealed that Ray had been involved in the fight in which he had been viciously kicked while down, and his head repeatedly thumped against the wall. This was a story that Dorothy had failed to include in her version of events leading up to her husband's death, and suddenly the police were investigating a possible murder case and their chief suspect was immediately arrested – screen star Paul Kelly.

Born in Brooklyn of Irish stock, Paul Kelly began acting in movies at the age of seven. His father was a saloon owner and his establishment was close to the Vitagraph Studios, which was very handy for the studio workers. They began borrowing furniture from Kelly to use on their sets, and one day in 1907 Mrs Kelly insisted that, in return for the favours she and her husband had shown, the studio give their small son an acting job. They put him into a picture, *A Good Little Devil*, and paid him five dollars a day.

As young Paul grew to an athletic six feet, he continued acting, both in films and on Broadway. Among his movies was *Anne of Green Gables* in which he co-starred with Mary Miles Minter and was directed by the ill-fated William Desmond Taylor.

He became a friend of Mr and Mrs Ray Raymond when they came to Hollywood, where the industry was about to undergo a revolution. *The Jazz Singer* hadn't yet been publicly shown as the first 'Talking Picture' but already studios were experimenting with various sound techniques in preparation for the revolution that the wise few knew would come. Hoping for an early break in these 'Talkies', Ray Raymond and Dorothy MacKaye had headed West.

It wasn't long before they landed a spot in a Vitaphone short recreating for the camera and microphone one of their stage acts. Neither was it too long before they earned for themselves the reputation of being fast-livers and hard-drinkers. Paul Kelly was numbered among their equally hard-drinking friends. He willingly threw in with them and other party people, and they 'partied around' at Kelly's place, at their own home, at the house of director Lewis Milestone, and anywhere else where a good time was wanted and where the bootleg liquor flowed.

Eventually, the rumour spread that Paul Kelly and Dorothy MacKaye were lovers and Ray began complaining about 'that sonofabitch Irishman who's been trying to steal my wife'. It was on that evening of 16 April 1927, when Kelly, high on a quart of Scotch, phoned Raymond to discuss both the rumours and Ray's complaints. It quickly deteriorated into a slanging match between two men who were both hopelessly drunk. Ray dared Kelly to come and face him. It was an invitation the hot-blooded Irishman couldn't turn down.

Ray was alone when Kelly arrived, except for Ethel Lee and Valerie, Dorothy and Raymond's four-year-old daughter. Dorothy was out shopping. As the fists began flying, Dorothy's little dog yapped repeatedly, adding to the noise and chaos. Raymond was really no match for Kelly who was taller than Ray and had a twenty-five-pound advantage. Kelly pounded into the song-and-dance star who just kept coming back for more of the same treatment.

Kelly grabbed him by the throat, slapping his face over and over. Then he dragged him along the floor, knocking over a table, and began slamming Ray's head against the wall. Leaving Raymond lying in a bloodied heap, Kelly left.

Much later, Dorothy claimed that after the fight, Paul had apologized to Ray, who accepted the apology and said all was forgiven. Said Dorothy, 'They fought like two kids, but those guys really liked each other.'

She says that before her husband died, he regained consciousness and begged her not to let Paul's name get dragged into things.

'I've had lots of fights in my life,' he told her. 'This thing was just another stupid brawl – it was as much my fault as his. So keep Paul's name out of it.'

And that's exactly what she tried to do. But following Kelly's arrest, both Dorothy and Dr Sullivan were charged with compounding a felony by attempting to conceal the facts surrounding the death of Raymond.

Dorothy may not have been an actual witness to the brawl that the prosecution claimed resulted in Raymond's death, but to all intents she was the star witness. Hers was the husband who'd died, and the jury were anxious to know of her attitude towards both the deceased husband and the movie star who had been charged, not with murder now, but manslaughter. But Dorothy was determined not to allow her feelings for either man to sway the jury one way or the other and allow the press the scandal they were hoping for. She remained purposely distant throughout the proceedings.

What everyone really wanted to know was – was she in love with Paul Kelly who now sat apprehensively in court, unable to attend the premiere of his latest picture, *Special Delivery*?

With an air of defiance, she responded to the District Attorney's cross-examination by saying that Paul Kelly was nothing more to her than a good friend. It was true, she admitted, that she had 'partied around' with Kelly. The DA immediately seized upon her confession.

'Did you consider his attentions proper?' he asked.

'Why, yes,' she replied. 'Nobody thought anything of it.'

'And why not?'

'Hollywood is different,' she said. 'We accept violation of convention because it is all right for us.' She was suddenly in trouble, and she tried to explain herself. 'Professional people are less conventional, more sophisticated . . .'

'So unconventional,' interrupted the DA, 'that you kill when someone is in the way?'

The defence called its own witnesses to testify to Kelly's character, including Lewis Milestone who had no hesitation in commending Kelly. But the prosecution had a number of its own aces. One of them was the maid, Ethel Lee. She had found dozens of letters written by Kelly under Dorothy's mattress, and these letters were produced as evidence of Kelly's love for Dorothy. With such lines as 'I'm crazy about you' being read in court, the press had a field day with the gradually gathering scandal. But still there had been nothing to prove that anything improper had gone on between Paul Kelly and Raymond's widow. Until, that was, Kelly's Japanese houseboy, Teno Yobu, was called to the stand.

He told the court of pyjama parties at Kelly's apartment and of serving Dorothy and Paul with breakfast in bed, complete with aspirins and seltzer for the inevitable hangovers. It was damning evidence which the DA had produced, although Yobu's testimony had the whole court in hysterics over his difficulty in pronouncing words. Despite the outbursts of mirth, the jury were quick to make up their minds.

Dorothy was in a hotel room fending off the press when Kelly's lawyer phoned through with devastating news. Kelly had been convicted of manslaughter and had been sentenced to serve one to ten years in San Quentin, one of America' toughest prisons. Dorothy swayed in a faint, but caught herself and facing the hungry press eager for something sensational to quote, she whispered defiantly, 'Well, that's that!'

Paul Kelly could have appealed, which would have kept him out of San Quentin for a time and inside the Los Angeles County Jail. But he simply stated, 'I want to get it over with,' and submitted to his sentence.

Before being sent to San Quentin, Kelly was allowed out of jail, though in the custody of the sheriff, to arrange his business affairs at the home of a friend. Dorothy, meanwhile, was being tried for compounding a felony (the same charge against Dr Sullivan had been dropped), and her own liberty was at stake. But she gladly risked everything to go and see Kelly the day he was at his friend's home with the sheriff. While the owner of the house led the sheriff on a grand tour of the place, Paul and Dorothy were free for a while to sit alone and hold hands. They really were deeply in love, and yet they regretted the death of Ray Raymond which neither had wanted under any circumstances. She later revealed that her reason for seeing Kelly that day, despite the risk to her own liberty, was because 'I couldn't let him be sent up like that without trying to make him see that whatever has been done is done, but there is still a future for us. I wanted to give him hope and let him know that if I got out before him, I'd be waiting for him.'

She had correctly predicted her own fate. The day after their last moments together it took the jury only two and a half hours to find Dorothy guilty. She was sentenced to one to three years, also at San Quentin.

She appealed against the sentence, fighting it for seven months. But she lost. 'Because I kept the promise I gave to my dying husband,' she said, 'a jury convicted me of compounding a felony.'

She was sent to the same prison as Kelly, yet they were unable to see each other. She occupied her time by organizing a drama club for the women prisoners and succeeded in putting on a play in the prison, becoming something of a confidante for fellow inmates. They watched how she went about designing and making fashionable outfits from her denim uniforms, and she began advising her companions on their own wardrobe, such as it was. Such was her warmth that the women felt easy in her presence and often poured out their hearts to her.

Before her first year inside was over, she was paroled for good behaviour.

Paul Kelly, meanwhile, had been keeping his nose clean behind bars. He lived in the hope of reconstructing his career when he got out, and he readied himself for the talking screen by taking elocution lessons and studying the whole technique of sound movies. He kept busy and made the time pass more easily. It paid off. After just a little more than two years he was paroled for good behaviour. Dorothy was true to her promise. She was waiting for him, and they married in 1931.

Kelly wasted no time in looking for work in the movies. He had tremendous drive and will power, and again his sense of purpose paid dividends. By 1932 he was back in motion pictures and went on to make scores of films, playing leads in B-pictures and good supporting roles in major films. More often than not, he played policemen and prison wardens and, occasionally, gangsters.

For once Hollywood had shown it could forgive someone who had broken the rules.

Dorothy was driving home to the ranch that she and Kelly owned near Northridge in the San Fernando Valley. It was 5 January 1940, and in the space of ten years the Kellys had prospered and their marriage blossomed. They were a happy family, completed by Valerie, Dorothy's daughter by Ray Raymond who was now a teenager. Not only had Paul's career taken off with a vengeance, but Dorothy had done well for herself too. She had turned her hand to writing plays, and her first, *Women In Prison*, had been successfully produced in 1932. It had, of course, been based not only on Dorothy's own experience but also on the experiences of those other women in prison who had so often loosened up and confided in her while she was in San Quentin. A year after the play was produced, Warner Bros. had turned it into a hit movie, *Ladies They Talk About*, starring Barbara Stanwyck. It would be remade in 1942 as *Lady Gangster*, but Dorothy was not destined to see it.

As she drove home that evening in 1940, her car suddenly skidded on a soft shoulder, spun out of control and turned over three times. Inside the crushed wreck Dorothy was pinned behind the wheel. She died, aged thirty-seven.

In 1947 Paul Kelly made a brilliant come-back to the theatre in the long-running production of William Wister Haines's *Command Decision*, for which he won the Tony Award, the Variety Critics' Award and the Donaldson Award. He continued making movies, appearing opposite John Wayne in *The High and the Mighty*, Gary Cooper in De Mille's *The Story of Dr. Wassell* and Tony Curtis in *The Square Jungle*, to name but a few.

He continued to work right up until 6 November 1956 when he died of a heart attack, aged fifty-seven.

CASE 4

Thelma Todd: The Ice Cream Blonde

HIGH ABOVE the Pacific Highway on the Palisades, between Santa Monica and Malibu, a garage door closed. Inside the garage was a Packard convertible, its top down, its engine running, its deadly exhaust fumes filling the air. In the front seat someone was slumped over, face down, lungs void of oxygen, heart stilled. She was – had been – Thelma Todd, Hollywood's 'Ice Cream Blonde', the zany dame of countless two-reel comedies for Hal Roach, and leading lady to the likes of Laurel and Hardy and the Marx Brothers.

The engine purred on until, finally, every drop of gasoline had been drunk by the Packard. The once dizzy, vivacious, wise-cracking Thelma was silent, still. Her blonde curls were matted. Her skin grew pale. Her porcelain replacement tooth had been knocked from her mouth. Blood spattered her face and evening gown, and spotted the mink coat which still hugged her shoulders.

That's how she was found on the morning of Monday, 16 December 1935, in the garage belonging to movie director Roland West. The police were called. Photographs of Thelma still lying slumped over were taken. The local residents were questioned, as was Roland West who was Thelma's current live-in lover. No one had seen her, it seemed, since she had come home early Sunday morning from a party at the Trocadero.

Sometime early that Sunday morning, reported the coroner, Thelma had died, choking on the exhaust fumes from the car. Suicide was a possibility, although no last note was found. The morning her body was found she was expected at the Roach Studios where she was starring with Laurel and Hardy in *The Bohemian Girl*. She had been Stan Laurel's choice as their leading lady. Now it would have to be completed without her. At the age of just thirty, she was already Hollywood history.

She was born on 29 July 1905, in Lawrence, Massachusetts. She may have been blonde, but she wasn't dumb: she had excelled at school and when she left she became a teacher. When she realized that her beauty could earn her more money than her brains, though, she took to modelling part-time.

Winning a beauty contest at the age of twenty, she attracted Hollywood talent scouts who were always lurking around beauty competitions on the lookout for potential talent, and the most evident talent had to be in looks.

Unlike many other such contest winners, Thelma didn't end up on the streets of Hollywood, disappointed, disillusioned and desperate enough to resort to prostitution or starring in stag movies. There were far too many good-looking girls seeking fame and fortune in Hollywood but finding only that a good pair of legs, an hourglass figure and a pretty face were not enough to get their names on a movie contract.

Paramount obviously felt that Thelma had the makings of a movie star, and they put her under contract in 1925 and made her one of their first pupils at their brand-new acting school at the studio. There they groomed and dressed and trained her for the silver screen. And they weren't prepared to give her so much as a walk-on part until they felt she was ready for it. Finally, after almost a year of learning to walk and talk and dance and sing, Thelma landed her first role, a small part, in *Fascinating Youth*, which starred her classmate, Charles 'Buddy' Rogers.

Throughout 1927 the studio continued to place her carefully in supporting roles in good feature films, such as *Rubber Heels* with Ed Wynn and *Nevada*, a western starring Gary Cooper.

Then Al Jolson spoke a few magic words from the screen in *The Jazz Singer* and the motion picture was suddenly revolutionized. The industry went through a harrowing metamorphosis as 'Talkies' became the new medium instead of being the flash in the pan so many people in movies had expected them to be.

Suddenly, some of the biggest names in movies vanished. John Gilbert, Clara Bow, Marie Provost, Roman Novarro, Billie Dove, Norma Talmadge and even newcomer Charles 'Buddy' Rogers were all forced into retirement as the public failed to respond to their voices. For many it was an overnight death. For a few others their demise spanned a few difficult years. A great many, unable to cope with their fall from grace, took their own lives. Some, such as John Gilbert, simply drank themselves to death. Now that Prohibition was no longer in force, liquor was consumed by the gallon.

For Thelma Todd the coming of sound allowed her to develop her wise-cracking screen persona, and the demise of many veterans made room for her to take a stab at stardom along with a whole new generation of actors who were theatrically trained and could use the talking pictures to full advantage.

In 1929 Thelma came to Hal Roach who featured her and comedy actress Zasu Pitts in a successful series of two-reelers. Although feature films had long superseded the short films that began the motion picture business, two-reel comedies were still in demand as supports, and Hal Roach was at this time the master of the two-reeler.

He had begun his film career as a stunt man and extra in Universal westerns. When he inherited $3,000 he formed his own company in 1915 and put his first actor under contract – Harold Lloyd, whom he had befriended when they were both unknowns at Universal.

But Roach's company was short-lived and while Lloyd went to work for Sennett at Keystone, Roach turned to directing movies for Essanay. He quickly proved his skill at conceiving and developing comic situations and putting them on to film, and somehow managed to persuade Pathé to sponsor him in forming another of his own companies. Harold Lloyd returned to him and began to emerge as a major comedy talent in a series of two-reelers directed by Roach.

While Mack Sennett emphasized slapstick, Roach concentrated on story, and the sophisticated audiences of the late Twenties and early Thirties displayed their preference for Roach's style over Keystone's at the box-office. As his success increased and his output of films grew, he called in other directors to take the load while he concentrated on supervision.

His biggest stars were Laurel and Hardy, Edgar Kennedy, Charlie Chase and Thelma Todd. She proved a real asset. As well as being a star of her own pictures, she also filled in well to support Stan and Ollie and Edgar Kennedy in their own series. She was with Laurel and Hardy in their very first 'talkie', *Unaccustomed As We Are* in 1929, in which she becomes the victim of the famous 'triple formula' which Stan Laurel and writer Leo McCarey had together devised. The first gag comes when Stan tries to light the gas and blows up the apartment. The second was Thelma, as the neighbour, rushing in to investigate the explosion and having her dress set on fire. Stan and Ollie tear the clothes off of her, leading to the 'topper' when Thelma's husband, Edgar Kennedy, returns home at the same time as Mrs Hardy. Poor Thelma, half-naked and almost burned to death, is stuffed into a trunk by Stan and Ollie.

As well as starring in her own two-reelers and supporting other comedy actors in theirs, she also played major roles in feature films for other studios. They were mostly comedies which allowed her to portray the wise-cracking cynical blonde that she personified. She was much in demand by major stars, and in 1931 the Marx Brothers had her playing a gangster in *Monkey Business*, and followed that by having her back again in *Horse Feathers*.

Stan Laurel always looked for opportunities to have her in his films. (He was, as is well known now, the creative force behind the Laurel and Hardy success.) But her brassy mannerisms made it difficult to fit her in with the majority of Laurel and Hardy pictures. But in 1933 Stan found a major role for her in *Fra Diavolo* (also called *The Devil's Brother*) based on Frank Auber's operetta. Jeannie MacPherson, Cecil B. De Mille's scenario writer, adapted the story, but Stan was unhappy with the treatment and was in constant contention with Roach throughout filming. Thelma frequently attempted to cheer him up, and often he responded to her bawdy sense of humour. She suffered from boyfriend difficulties, and she'd confide in Stan, relating her latest romantic misadventures, and the two of them would fall about laughing.

The film turned out to be the most commercially successful Laurel and Hardy feature, and during the 1960s it was reissued in Europe to smash business.

In 1933 Thelma had the extraordinary experience of being directed by William Wyler in *Counsellor-At-Law*. Wyler always had the reputation of being a hard task-master with actors, and his films usually went way over budget and schedule, usually resulting in first-class pictures. This movie was no exception, and it served to enforce Thelma's public image and popularity in her own two-reelers.

Zasu Pitts had gone her own way in 1930 and Thelma had been joined by Patsy Kelly, and the series had continued to prove successful. By 1935 the Thelma Todd and Patsy Kelly comedies were still going strong, the two girls playing off their contrasting personalities to great effect. Patsy portrayed the same kind of wise-cracking girl as Thelma, but she had a seemingly inevitable trend towards disaster, and she was as dowdy as Thelma was glamorous.

While Thelma's career was hitting the high spots, her private life, perhaps typically, was always in trouble. She had, for a time, been married to Pat DiCicco, and since her divorce had had numerous affairs. In 1931 she had made a picture, *Corsair*, co-starring with Chester Morris. It was directed by Roland West. He was married to actress Jewel Carmen, but in true Hollywood tradition, he moved in with Thelma.

West's involvement with Thelma, and her tragic end, would prove to be more than just a personal blow for West.

Roland West had earned the respect of Hollywood. His output as a director and occasional producer was small, but his work was highly appreciated for the atmosphere he created.

His talent extended to writing, and his 1923 production, *The Unknown Purple*, was adapted from his own stage play. One of his greatest successes came in 1926 with *The Bat* which featured Jack Pickford, Louise Fazenda and his wife Jewel Carmen.

His visually impressive *The Dove*, made in 1928 and starring Norma Talmadge and Gilbert Roland, won an Aacademy Award for its art director William Cameron Menzies. It showed West's typical demand for visual flair to help create atmosphere.

His 1931 picture, *The Bat Whispers*, with Chester Morris, was acclaimed as one of the most extraordinary thrillers ever filmed. Yet, despite his success, he rarely directed more than one film a year, although in 1931 he did make a second, *Corsair*. In doing so he walked out on his wife and took up with his cute, blonde leading lady, Thelma Todd.

Together, Thelma and West opened up a business, 'Thelma

Todd's Roadside Rest' café. It sat nestling under the Palisades on the Pacific Highway. Many of their famous friends frequented the place and it became a popular hang-out for star-struck fans.

There were living quarters above the café; separate apartments for Thelma and West, but connected by sliding doors. West also maintained a grand house on Pasetano Road, tucked away behind Sunset Boulevard at the point where it hits the sea at the Pacific Highway. It was only a climb up many steps from the restaurant.

It seems that the affair had been petering out for some time. When they had first met she was twenty-six and he forty-four. Now she was still young at thirty but he was ageing at forty-eight. She still had what she considered a zest for life. Probably figuring that you're only young once, she was out to make the best of what years of young womanhood she had left. Mistaking fast living for a fulfilled life, she drank a great deal, took pills and cheated on West.

Whatever vices she may have had, though, she did not want any part of underworld activity, which was on offer to her. California had not yet become part of the gangster empire which ran many of America's other states and big cities. Bootlegging during Prohibition and drug trafficking had been rife in Hollywood, but the West Coast had by and large remained untouched by the underworld.

However, at this time Lucky Luciano was making an attempt to penetrate California with his illegal gambling enterprise. He had casinos all over the country, and with so much money flowing in and around Los Angeles, Luciano was intent on pioneering this new land. He was constantly on the lookout for establishments from which he could run his illegal gambling joints, and Thelma Todd's Roadside Rest seemed to be the perfect front.

He paid her a visit one day. But face to face with Lucky Luciano, one of the biggest of the mobsters, Thelma proved she was just as gutsy off screen as she was on. He made her what he considered a generous offer. He wanted to transform the upper storey of the café into a secret casino. All she had to do was to keep the business flowing by escorting her rich and famous friends upstairs to try their luck at the gambling tables. He promised her she would be well rewarded.

She turned him down flat.

Thelma didn't always get the prime roles, but she often managed to steal every scene she was in. In 1935 she appeared with Bing Crosby in a Paramount musical *Two For Tonight*. But it was really a vehicle for Bing to croon to Joan Bennett while Thelma specialized as usual in providing the well-delivered wise-cracks.

In November she began work with Laurel and Hardy again, in the feature-length musical *The Bohemian Girl*. By now Stan and Ollie had virtually given up making two-reelers as Laurel wanted to concentrate on features. Thelma and Patsy Kelly were still turning out their short comedies and were happy to go on doing so.

Like *Fra Diavolo*, *The Bohemian Girl* was based on an operetta. Stan found an unusual role for Thelma to play: a Gypsy Queen's daughter. With a dark wig covering her platinumed hair, she filmed the opening sequence in which she sang a stirring Gypsy song.

She continued to work on the film well into December and by 14 December, when she was one of many guests at a Hollywood party, she was still shooting scenes.

The party was thrown by Ida Lupino, a relative newcomer to Hollywood, having been born in England where she began her movie career in 1933. She was actually only seventeen years old, and the party was probably masterminded by her studio, Paramount, hiring the whole of the Trocadero for the big event.

That Saturday night party had all the classic ingredients for an explosive Hollywood ball. Thelma's ex-husband, Pat DiCicco, was there with actress Margaret Lindsay, and inevitably as Thelma's alcohol consumption rose, she and DiCicco exchanged some heated words during the evening.

The party swung on into the early hours of Sunday morning by which time Thelma had had more than her usual amount of booze. At least she didn't have to drive home; she had a chauffeur-driven car which whisked her back.

Roland West was at the apartment over the café and received a phone call from theatre-owner Sid Grauman saying that Thelma was a bit 'under the influence' and on her way home. Grauman suggested that West see her safely into bed.

Sometime between then and the morning of 16 December, Thelma Todd died in the garage at West's house on Pasetano Road.

The morning that she was found by her maid, Stan and Ruth Laurel received a Christmas card from Thelma. Her death had stunned Stan and shocked Roach who always tried to maintain a virtuous image for his actresses. Throughout the week Christmas gifts that she had sent out continued to arrive at the homes of her friends, including Stan Laurel's.

On the following Monday she was laid to rest at Forest Lawn. A huge crowd gathered to view the open casket in which she lay blanketed by yellow roses. Patsy Kelly was there mourning her screen partner; she was soon to continue their special brand of comedy with a new side-kick, Lydia Roberti. Zasu Pitts also paid her last respects. She noted how well the funeral arrangers had made Thelma up. 'Why, she looked as if she was going to sit up and talk,' she later noted.

If only she could have talked. The inquest on her death begged for answers that maybe only she could have ever fully given.

Had Thelma killed herself?

It was not too uncommon for suicide to be effected by car exhaust fumes in the enclosed space of a garage – but then again, neither was it uncommon for killers to murder people in the same fashion.

If she had killed herself, how did she come to have blood over her face and clothes? Those who commit suicide nearly always leave a note, but no suicide note was ever found from Thelma.

And why, as many of her friends asked, would she come home in a chauffeur-driven limousine, then climb all those steps up the cliffside to West's garage, just to kill herself when it was known by all her friends that she kept a plentiful supply of pills which she could have overdosed on?

Some of these questions were to be covered at the inquest, and a galaxy of witnesses was brought forward.

Guests from Ida Lupino's party, including Lupino herself, were questioned. All agreed that Thelma had drunk a lot more than usual, and although she seemed her normal carefree self throughout the party, she was in a morose mood when she left for home.

Ida Lupino told the court how Thelma confided in her that she was having an affair with a wealthy businessman from San Francisco, but Lupino had no idea of the identity of this new lover.

Sid Grauman explained how he had called Roland West to inform him of Thelma's drunken state and had suggested he made sure she got to bed safely.

Witnesses from the neighbourhood told the court how they had seen Thelma, still in her evening gown and mink coat, screaming obscenities and kicking at the door of her apartment.

West was called to testify, and he admitted that instead of helping Thelma to bed that early Sunday morning, he had locked the doors. He also confessed that they had had a furious row, but he never did give an adequate explanation as to why he had bolted the doors to both apartments so that Thelma couldn't get in.

He added a strange twist to his testimony. He said that he had heard his dog barking around 3.30 a.m. and shortly after had heard water running in Thelma's apartment. He assumed from that that she had managed to get indoors.

An examination of the door did reveal marks where it seemed it had been kicked. But police were baffled as to how anyone could have gained entrance to the apartment if, as West had claimed, the door had been bolted from the inside.

Suspicions against West were quickly raised. A remarkable theory was formed. West would have staged the whole scene by hiring some hard-on-her-luck girl to dress in Thelma's clothes and then stand outside and scream and kick at the door for all to see, while inside he beat the real Thelma into unconsciousness.

Had West found out about her affair with the man from San Francisco and killed her in a jealous rage? And if that were true, had he in planning the murder created a seemingly perfect alibi by having witnesses actually see a Thelma lookalike locked out of their apartments, thus proving him innocent?

There was still the suicide theory to conjure with. If West had in reality locked her out and she had been drunk and morose, then she would, if suicide had been her plan, have been unable to get to those pills of hers. A long climb up to the garage would then seem feasible. But that did not explain the fact that she had been roughed up.

If it had been suicide, why would she have killed herself because of a lover's tiff if she had been about to break up with West anyway for another man?

What other kind of personal problems did she have that could possibly have driven her to take her own life?

Zasu Pitts revealed at the inquest that she had lent thousands of dollars to Thelma which she had poured into her restaurant business. Zasu had never received a single dime back.

Vast debts had often driven people to suicide, but Zasu, although no longer working with Thelma, was still a close friend and never pressurized Thelma to repay the loan.

The suicide theory refused to stick, and finally no one who knew her believed that she had taken her own life. But it was equally difficult to pin down who could have murdered her.

Roland West seemed to have a strong alibi, although his story was contradictory, claiming to have locked her out and that later he had heard her in her own apartment. He was, by his own admission about the argument, the last known person to speak with her on that Sunday morning, and it was shortly after, the police believed, that Thelma died.

And then came a surprising testimony by West's wife, Jewel Carmen, which put the whole case into further turmoil. She claimed that she had seen Thelma on Sunday morning when the sun was up, driving her Packard past the intersection of Hollywood and Vine. At her side had sat a handsome stranger. Yet the police and the coroner had been convinced that Thelma had died in the early hours of Sunday.

How reliable a witness was Jewel Carmen? She was West's wife. He was a prime suspect in the case. If her testimony was true, it seemed unlikely that West could have killed her, since the theory was that it had to have happened after Thelma returned from the party.

Was Jewel Carmen protecting her husband? He had not lived with her for a long time, and as far as he was concerned his marriage was over. Why would a jilted wife protect her two-timing husband? Many questions arise over Jewel Carmen's testimony. Were she and West in on the whole thing? Did she still love him enough to protect him? Or was she simply telling the truth?

Whatever the facts behind it, Jewel's story threw the jury into total confusion. They spent weeks deliberating all the evidence, much of it contradictory. Eventually they announced their verdict.

'Death due to carbon monoxide poisoning.'

That was all they could conclude, and the case was closed.

But Thelma's lawyer, who attended the inquest, had always thought that the wrong route had been taken. He didn't believe for a minute that Thelma had killed herself. Nor did he believe that Roland West was responsible. He believed that he could pin the murder on Lucky Luciano. He prevailed upon the District Attorney for a second inquest at which, he claimed, he would prove his theory.

His belief was that when Thelma Todd had turned down Luciano's deal, she had, in effect, signed her own death warrant. Lucky Luciano was not the kind of man to reveal his illicit plans unless he felt sure that whoever knew them would remain silent. If he couldn't buy them off, he would bump them off. It seemed perfectly logical to this lawyer that Luciano had no intention of taking any risks as far as Thelma Todd was concerned.

But when Hal Roach heard about the second inquest and the lawyer's theory, he begged the District Attorney to drop the matter. At the mere mention of Luciano's name, Roach turned white. He was certainly no Adolph Zukor; he did not command the same kind of power and authority. He didn't' possess the means to organize a cover-up. All he could do was to try and persuade the lawyer that they would all be better off if the inquest didn't go ahead. Reluctantly, the Attorney agreed. Consequently, the murder of Thelma Todd was never solved.

Laurel and Hardy finished making *The Bohemian Girl* later in December. During January Stan worked on its editing with Bert Jordan. As Laurel watched the images of Thelma flash before him, he felt disturbed that she should still be so funny even though she was gone.

Out of nothing more than respect for her, he deleted most of her scenes. He believed that to leave them in would simply be morbid. It was ironic that in her last film, The Ice-Cream Blonde was seen, albeit briefly, in a dark wig.

Although the case had been wrapped up as far as the law was concerned, too many questions remained unanswered and, as usual, involvement in the affair was enough to bring about Hollywood's own style of retribution. The industry had already proved that it could terminate the careers of those in its employ with Mabel Normand, Mary Miles Minter and Roscoe Arbuckle. Now Hollywood closed its studio doors to Roland West. He never worked again.

But not everyone in the business believed that West had had any connection with Thelma's death. They smelt, as did Thelma's lawyer, a strong underworld connection, though none dared publicly admit it. As law and order had increased on that last Western frontier, so too had organized crime. The mobsters were already making inroads, and Lucky Luciano was in discreet evidence. The mobsters didn't yet have the kind of control they wanted over Hollywood, but that was soon to change. Obviously, nobody in the business was going to claim that Mr Luciano had killed Thelma.

But it was strongly implied in private. According to David Niven in his book *Bring On the Empty Horses*, Clark Gable had told him that Thelma Todd had been 'knocked off by gangsters'.

It was certainly enough to ensure that the stars and moguls of Hollywood learned to treat Mr Luciano and his colleagues with respect and caution. They figured they knew what could happen to them if they didn't.

But it was too late to warn Thelma Todd.

Bugsy Siegel: George Raft's Blue-eyed Buddy

THE HOUSE AT 810 Linden Drive in Beverly Hills looked for all the world like a Spanish-Moorish castle. It was a strange quirk of fashionable Beverly Hills designers that no house should look as if it was simply built to be lived in: each had to be a status symbol. There were houses that looked as though they belonged in the pages of Tudor history, Roman history, and even the pages of the Arabian Nights.

The occupant of the Moorish house was Virginia Hill. She didn't own it, she just rented it, and she could afford to. She may have been only a small-time actress, but she was a big-time gangster's moll. Her connections with the underworld were widely known. She had used her dark beauty to elevate her from hostess at underworld parties to supporting actress in movies. But the big money wasn't in acting.

She had been working for, and falling in and out of love with, the charming king of the Hollywood underworld, Benjamin 'Bugsy' Siegel. His tanned handsome face, highlighted by blue eyes, had, for the past decade, been as familiar to the film colony as that of any movie star. But his dealings in the movie world and in the gambling casinos of Las Vegas were not the type that Louella Parsons or Hedda Hopper cared, nor dared, to mention in their columns.

He liked to think that he had friends among the Hollywood community. Indeed, he had one sure friend, George Raft, who epitomized the Gangster on screen. But everyone else simply tolerated him for their own good, as the memory of Thelma Todd still burned bright.

Yet Siegel, for all his ungodly rackets, had such a charm about him that when he had first arrived in Hollywood eleven years earlier people warmed to him.

Right now, though, Virginia was decidedly cool on him. There had been a row, and she simply handed him the keys to her home and then left with a rich French boy half her age for a vacation in Europe.

So she was not at home on the night of 29 June 1947. It was almost midnight as Siegel, lonely and aching for Virginia, sat on the couch in her living room reading the newspaper. Insomnia was, to any racketeer, an occupational hazard.

Suddenly the window splintered into a thousand fragments. Bullets peppered the far wall. He didn't even have the chance to dive to the floor. His head exploded with machine-gun bullets. He simply slumped over where he sat, his blue eyes blasted into blood-soaked sockets.

In front of him, on a table, a small statuette of a naked woman with her arms raised seemed to be making the proclamation that the king of the Hollywood underworld was dead, and there was no one but George Raft to mourn him.

Trying to find out who had killed him was not going to be easy for the police. He had hundreds of enemies whom he'd earned on his long climb up from street punk to mob leader. He was hardly more than fifty when he died, but he was a million years away from his boyhood in the slums of New York and his misspent youth during the Great Depression.

They were just teenage kids, trying to escape the grim, rat-infested area of New York called appropriately Hell's Kitchen. The Depression was on, and Bugsy Siegel and his pal George Raft knew there was more than one way to skin a cat.

The problem with Raft was that he was lazy. He didn't want to work. He figured he could make money the easy way. There were plenty of mobs who might take in a kid with promise like his. He could certainly take care of himself. He could box, and had graduated from the gymnasium to the prize-ring where he could boast of winning fifteen of his twenty-two bouts. He also managed to leave the ring without too much damage to his Valentino looks.

He needed his looks when he became a dance-hall gigolo, moving in on the older wealthy women who were willing to pay a handsome young man like Raft to keep them company. He could dance pretty well, too – nobody could do the Charleston

Thelma Todd, the 'Ice Cream Blonde' (*above*) in *Counsellor-At-Law*, one of her best pictures, and (*below*) with Antonio Moreno in *The Bohemian Girl*, for which she wore a dark wig. Much of her work was subsequently cut out of this film, which had not been completed at the time of her mysterious death in 1935.

George Raft (*left*), seen here with C. Henry Gordon in *Scarface*.

Paul Kelly (*above right*), was convicted of murder in 1927 — but went on working in movies afterwards. (*Below, left to right*) Kelly, Jim Backus, Tony Curtis, Ernest Borgnine, in *The Square Jungle* (1956).

Lana Turner with her three-year-old daughter Cheryl who, in 1958, at the age of fourteen, would kill her mother's lover, Johnny Stompanato.

Lana Turner in *Another Time Another Place* (1958), with a young Sean Connery.

The murder of actress LaJean Ethridge in 1959 caused problems for John Wayne in the making of *The Alamo*, which he produced, directed and starred in.

faster than he.

In this racket, he elevated himself through clubs in London and back in New York again until he scored really big by dancing on the Broadway stage with partner Elsie Pilcer. In turn, that led to him dancing in numerous shows such as *Gay Paree*, *No Foolin'*, *Palm Beach Nights* and *City Chap*.

But if anyone should mistake his dancing talents as a sign of getting soft, then he could always flash the gun that he carried when he was off the stage doing dirty work for racketeer Owney Maddon who did a nice line in bootleg liquor. Being part of Maddon's gang meant more to Raft than being a showboy.

'If I had any ambition,' he once said, 'it was to be a big shot in my pal Owney Maddon's liquor mob. I had a gun in my pocket, and I was cocky because I was working for the gang boss of New York.'

Maddon never underestimated Raft's strength and fighting skill. When cowgirl movie star Texas Guinan asked Maddon to supply a protection crew for her nightclub, the gang boss included Raft in the squad of gangsters.

When Guinan saw Raft, she was impressed enough with his looks to suggest that he come to Hollywood and play a small part in her new picture, *Queen of the Clubs*. All of a sudden he was an actor with no training, but he managed his part well. Then he was sitting one day in the Brown Derby when director Rowland Brown spotted him.

He asked him who he was and what he was doing. Raft explained he'd just played a small part in Guinan's movie.

Brown said, 'I've got another small part you can play.' And the next thing Raft knew, he was appearing in *Quick Millions* as a hood. It was a cinch for him.

Further movie roles followed, then in 1932 he appeared with Paul Muni in Howard Hawks's gangster classic, *Scarface*. Paramount now took an interest in him and signed him to a contract. By 1936 he was one of Hollywood's biggest stars and was giving Paramount the run-around by walking out on *The Princess Comes Across* because he didn't like leading lady Carole Lombard's choice of cameraman. His antics didn't prevent the studio from raising his weekly salary to $4,000.

It was about then that Bugsy Siegel rode into town.

While Raft had been making good money from rich old women on the dance floor, Benjamin 'Bugsy' Siegel was proving himself to be a real punk; he raped girls, single-handedly burgled homes, and generally let everyone know that they couldn't push him around.

His beginnings in organized crime came when he pushed heroin for Lucky Luciano, then, during Prohibition, he ran bootleg liquor for Meyer Lansky. With his good looks and boyish charm, he quickly became a ladies' man, so that rape was no longer necessary. There were plenty of Broadway showgirls queueing up to be his moll, if only for a night.

When New York gangland leaders learned that a Chicago mob was planning to move in on Hollywood and the movie business, Siegel and half a dozen other gangsters were chosen to get there ahead of the Chicago boys. It was 1936 and tinsel town was still wide open to all possibilities. Not nearly half its racketeering potential had by then been realized. Bugsy arrived in Hollywood with an ace up his sleeve.

That was his old pal George Raft.

Raft had not broken his connections with the underworld, and he was ready for Siegel when he arrived. Bugsy was able to rent the mansion belonging to singing movie star Lawrence Tibbett.

There was gold to be made in Hollywood in rackets that just couldn't be run anywhere else. Studios hired extras by the hundred for many movies – westerns, historical sagas, even contemporary dramas all had their uses for extras. Siegel and his henchmen moved in to shake down both the studios and the extras. If the extras wanted to work, they had to pay Siegel for the privilege. As for the studio heads, if they wanted the extras, they also had to pay up or find that there were no extras at all who were willing to cross Siegel and turn up for work.

Siegel made half a million dollars in one year from this, pouring his profits into the equally lucrative investments of drugs and slave trafficking.

Raft was happy to help his pal get to know those in Hollywood who could unwittingly help him along. All Bugsy had to do was to smile and let his blue eyes shine, and he seemed to mingle perfectly with the movie crowd, getting on well with the likes of

Clark Gable, Jean Harlow, Gary Cooper and Cary Grant. These movie stars were very careful how they treated Siegel. He may have been warm, friendly and delighted to be numbered among the rich and famous of Hollywood, but they all remembered Thelma Todd and were not about to chance offending the smiling gangster.

He courted numerous actresses, but the one he really wanted wouldn't have him – Jean Harlow. He paid her much attention which she tolerated but refused to allow herself to be swept off her feet by his immense charm. It also irked her that her shady step-father Marino Bello began getting involved in Bugsy's rackets. It seems Siegel was infatuated enough with Harlow to put up with her rejection of his advances. He remained fond of her up to her death in 1937. He was there when they buried her, publicly displaying his undying affection for the platinum blonde. It seemed a genuinely touching gesture, although he turned up at many film stars' funerals.

Despite his enchantment with Hollywood personalities, he continued to milk the town for all it was worth with numerous 'businesses'. Then, in 1939, it seemed to all that he was at last to get his just deserts when he was indicted, along with several others, for the murder of stool-pigeon Harry Greenberg. Word had got out that Greenberg was about to squeal on his friends, and consequently he was silenced before the police had dealt with him.

Siegel was put in jail and denied bail, but he was able to ensure that his time behind bars was not entirely devoid of luxury.

The guard slapped the handcuffs on Siegel and led him from his cell. They stepped outside and into a waiting car. Bugsy looked his usual dapper self and, although manacled, continued to pour on the charm. He could afford to smile. This was his day out. His money could buy him just about anything he wanted.

They pulled up outside Lindy's Wilshire Boulevard Café, and Siegel stepped out, his attached guard on tow. Inside the plush café, they found the men's cloakroom. There the guard unlocked the cuffs and Siegel's arms were free to embrace his waiting girlfriend, actress Wendy Barrie. Later that day Siegel duly returned to his patient guard who slipped the cuffs back on and led him back to his cell.

During the one and a half months he was 'inside', he enjoyed eighteen such outings. As for the charges brought against him, attorney Jerry Geisler got him off. Thereafter, Jerry Geisler became the most sought-after lawyer in Hollywood, and in ensuing years he successfully defended Errol Flynn on a charge of statutory rape, and he represented Charlie Chaplin in a scandalous paternity suit. Whenever movie stars found themselves in trouble with the law, they usually called for the brilliant Jerry Geisler, the man who had helped Bugsy Siegel to go free.

But perhaps Siegel's acquittal wasn't entirely due to Geisler's skill. It certainly couldn't have hurt Bugsy's chances in court when he donated $50,000 to the re-election campaign of Los Angeles District Attorney Dockweiler!

Virginia Hill, affectionately known as 'Sugar', was a beautiful brunette with a talent for wheeling and dealing. She'd left her home town of Alabama to see where fortune would lead her in the vice dens of New York.

She came to the attention of Lucky Luciano and fellow mobster Frank Costello, and earned great sums by playing hostess at some of their lavish parties. She was a real moll, playing her charms for all they were worth against the desires of her Mafia boyfriends.

As Hollywood's underworld activities grew under the direction of Bugsy Siegel, she packed her bags and headed West in 1941 to tread new ground and even try her luck in the movies. It wasn't long before she was hanging affectionately on the arm of Siegel, and he pulled a few nervous strings and landed her a role in Sam Goldwyn's *Ball of Fire*. The picture starred Gary Cooper, Barbara Stanwyck and Dana Andrews, and was directed by Howard Hawks who had turned another hood into a star when he directed George Raft in *Scarface*.

Ball of Fire didn't exactly do the same thing for Virginia, but the picture was a huge success. At the glittering premiere, all the stars were there, and among them was Virginia, accompanied by boyfried Bugsy, the biggest shot in town. He enjoyed his association with the movie stars and had a ball at the party that followed the premiere. But still people were simply playing safe by not offending the man.

By this time Siegel even had a wife, but she stayed out of the picture, content to live off the fat of the land that her womanizing husband supplied. He, meantime, continued to accompany Virginia and was, all by accounts, more in love with her than with anyone else he had ever known.

Late in 1941 he again beat a rap, this time for bookmaking. George Raft offered himself as a character witness, as if Siegel needed one in that town.

'I've known Mr Siegel for twenty years,' said Raft from the stand. 'We have been friends for a long, long time.'

He was also one of Siegel's few remaining friends. As Bugsy had prospered and grown more powerful, he'd trodden on a lot of toes in the underworld.

Las Vegas, in 1944, was just a sleepy, aged town in the middle of the dusty Nevada landscape. It had been preserved as a kind of memorial to the old frontier, and the mayor intended to keep it that way. But that year Bugsy Siegel passed through and was suddenly struck by a vision. He saw in his mind's eye a huge hotel which would house the biggest casino in the country. It would be a Mecca for gamblers, who would come from all over the world to play at his gambling tables.

He immediately set in motion the wheels that would see his dream become a reality. He went to a number of equally undesirable 'businessmen' and persuaded them to lend him several million dollars. It would be a tremendous investment for them and, although some of them had become his enemies, the sweet smell of money was enough to convince his colleagues that the investment was worth the gamble. But they made it plain that they intended to be repaid in full with interest.

In 1945 he purchased a piece of land on which stood a rundown hotel owned by a bankrupt widow who was only too pleased to be rid of it. The workmen moved in and demolished the hotel, and a new edifice began to rise, complete with several tons of Carrara marble which Luciano, now exiled to his homeland, managed to smuggle out.

By Christmas 1946, The Flamingo was ready to open. It had cost $6,000,000 and the 'investors' were eager to see a quick return. But business began slowly and Siegel was intent on keeping all initial profits for himself. His creditors would just have to wait. Meanwhile, he made plans to build on and develop more of Las Vegas, but during this time Virginia grew bored, and in the spring of 1947 she walked out on him and headed back to Los Angeles.

She found a huge Moorish mansion which she rented, and allowed herself to be wooed by a rich French youth who was only half her age. He promised to take her to Europe and she wasted no time in packing.

Before she could leave, Siegel tracked her down and was on her doorstep. He was desperate to have her back, but she had no intention of living in a dustbowl any longer. She wanted the civilized landscape of Beverly Hills and the Pacific Ocean to play in. He promised her he'd stay in Los Angeles. She dropped the keys of the house in his hand and told him she'd see him when she got back from Europe.

So Siegel stayed in Virginia's home, and on 20 June at midnight he was murdered.

It was the law's duty to investigate, though very few people in Hollywood were sorry to see him dead. This was one time when not a single person in the movie industry stood in the way of justice. But the investigation was complicated by the simple fact that Siegel had earned too many enemies, all of whom wanted him out of their way.

The police finally gave up and no indictments were made. However, it later came out that Siegel had been killed by hit-men hired by those who had invested in The Flamingo. They had not been repaid, and Siegel had made no attempt to placate his investors. So they made him pay in full.

He was buried in Beth Olam Cemetery near RKO's studios. Only a sparse gathering watched him lowered into the ground. He had often witnessed the funerals of movie stars, such was his affection for the demi-gods of Hollywood, but none turned up for his funeral. Not even George Raft who had remained his friend but who was now on his way down and couldn't make such a big noise in Hollywood any more.

Raft spent the next few years making pictures in Europe, but eventually Great Britain refused him a work permit because of his underworld connections, and towards the end of his life Britain barred him altogether. Even his own government began hounding him for unpaid taxes.

As his acting career declined, he followed in Bugsy's footsteps and opened up casinos in various countries, including Britain and Cuba. But Castro closed down the Havana casino without compensation, and once barred from the UK Raft never again stepped foot inside his plush London casino. He was an old man, somewhere in his eighties, when he died, outliving his pal Bugsy by more than thirty years, yet he never escaped that close association he was known to have had with Siegel, and allegations of underworld involvement stayed for ever with Raft.

But at least he didn't meet the violent end which terminated Bugsy Siegel, the Godfather of Hollywood with the baby-blue eyes.

CASE 6

Lana Turner's Tragic Valentine

CHIEF DETECTIVE ANDERSON could have been forgiven for forgetting that this was Good Friday. For the public it was a holiday, but the Los Angeles police department didn't close shop; crime didn't stop just because it was Easter. So it was that Anderson, accompanied by another detective, sped through town on their way to 730 North Bedford Drive, Beverly Hills late on 4 April 1958, to investigate a probable homicide at the home of screen goddess Lana Turner.

Arriving at the Moorish-styled Hollywood mansion, Anderson and his partner were led by police officers into a bedroom furnished with pink curtains, pink carpet and pink bed linen. On the floor lay the body of a man dressed in casual slacks, shirt and an open woollen cardigan. An officer knelt down and pulled up the shirt, revealing a stab wound in the stomach.

The corpse was that of Johnny Stompanato, better known as Johnny Valentine. He was certainly not unknown to the police. He had strong mob connections and his name had been linked to a number of famous actresses. Lana Turner had been the latest.

Lana Turner, the great screen beauty, stood over the body of the man she had loved. Her make-up ran with tears. Her famous bleached hair was a mess. Her thirty-seven years were ravaged by the trauma of this night.

She approached Police Chief Anderson. 'Can't I take the blame for this horrible thing?' she pleaded.

'Not unless you have committed the crime,' replied Anderson. 'We'll find out all the facts.'

The officers led Anderson and his partner into another bedroom. There waited Lana's fourteen-year-old daughter, Cheryl. She was tall for her age – five feet, eight inches – and she was tanned by the Californian sun. She was crying.

'I stabbed him,' she said. 'I didn't mean to kill him. I just meant to frighten him.'

Anderson knew Stompanato had been a tough character, and

88

he had some doubt that a girl as young as Cheryl could have killed such a man, obviously face to face. He was led to the bathroom where, in the sink, lay a bloodstained kitchen knife. It carried a nine-inch blade fashioned into an almost needle-sharp point. All of Anderson's doubts faded. With such a sleek, sharp weapon, it wouldn't have been difficult to kill Stompanato with one blow.

As Stompanato's body was carted off to the morgue for the inevitable post-mortem, the story of his death in the house of screen idol Lana Turner sent the wires buzzing across the country and the next morning the public was hearing it on radios, watching it on TV and reading it over breakfast.

Everyone, of course, knew who Lana Turner was, but few had heard of Johnny Stompanato. One who knew him well was gangster and gambler Mickey Cohen. He had on occasion hired gigolo Johnny Stompanato as a bodyguard. When he heard that Johnny was dead, Cohen said, 'This was a great guy.'

But when police summoned him to make a formal identification of the body, Cohen steadfastly refused 'on the grounds that I may be accused of this murder'.

Before the inquest opened, one enterprising newspaper editor approached Cohen and asked if he had any evidence of Lana Turner's love affair with Stompanato, such as any love letters. In no time at all Cohen managed to acquire a pile of Lana's letters to Stompanato which had been kept at the deceased's apartment. On 9 April, just two days before the inquest was due to take place, the American press splashed Lana's love letters all over their front pages. Once again the turbulent love life of Lana Turner, which never stayed buttoned up for too long, was laid bare, only this time in a sensational murder scandal. And the official investigation had hardly begun.

Accusations were flying about, and Lana was being put on trial by both the press and the public, and yet she hadn't even been charged with killing Stompanato. It was her daughter, Cheryl, who had confessed to the killing, but Lana was being held to blame and her morals condemned. Unable to see that this was a terrible tragedy in her life, everyone, it seemed, could think of the whole affair only as another lurid episode in the life of Lana Turner. Only when she appeared in court, shown live on television, did Mr and Mrs America come to understand.

But what no one at all could really begin to comprehend was the feeling of paralytic shock over the loss of a loved one under the most tragic of circumstances for the second time in her life. For many years earlier, Lana's father had been murdered.

The girl that the world came to know as Lana Turner began life as Judy Turner, born on 8 February 1921 in Wallace, Idaho. She had other names too in her pre-adolescent years, for the sole purpose of her and her parents avoiding the police. Her father, Virgil, was a bootlegger, a small-time crook, and he was continually adopting new names for himself and his wife Mildred and daughter Judy.

He'd tried to make an honest living as an insurance salesman, and his work took the family from town to town. But more than once he'd had to resort to digging in the mines or working on the docks to earn enough to live on. Finally he took to gambling and bootlegging.

Judy loved dad, and he was crazy about her. He could tap dance a bit, and taught her. But the hard life he was living led to a separation between him and Mildred, although they never divorced. They were living apart in San Francisco when, on 15 December 1930, Virgil was murdered in the street and his winnings from a poker game stolen.

Mildred found herself a job working in a beauty parlour, but her hours were so long that she sent Judy to live with friends of the family in Modesto, California. There she was cruelly treated and relegated to a servile position. When Mildred found out, she gave up her job and took Judy to Sacramento to look for another job while Judy attended a Catholic school run by the Dominican nuns. But when Mildred failed to find work, they returned to smog-bound San Francisco where Mildred's health suffered. Their doctor strongly advised them to take to the warmer, drier clime of Los Angeles.

So Judy was enrolled at Hollywood High School while mother found work in another beauty salon. The school was just a few blocks away from Hollywood and Vine. There were plenty of girls who dreamed of finding movie stardom. But Judy never even considered it.

Then one day in January 1936, she was perched on a stool at a soda fountain on Sunset Boulevard when the manager came over to her and, pointing to a man with a moustache, said, 'Judy, that's Mr Billy Wilkerson. He's a friend of mine. He's all right. He wants me to introduce him to you.'

'No,' said Judy, cautious that this would be nothing more than an attempted pick-up.

'Aw, come on, Judy,' said the manager. 'This ain't what you think it is.'

'No,' said Judy again. So Mr Wilkerson came over and introduced himself.

'I'm Billy Wilkerson, publisher of *The Hollywood Reporter*. How would you like to be in pictures?'

'No thanks.'

'I understand. You don't know anything about me. But suppose you take this card with my office address on it. Could you and your mother come to see me?'

That evening Judy told her mother what had happened. Mildred went straight out and bought a copy of *The Hollywood Reporter*, a leading trade magazine, and sure enough, it bore Mr Wilkerson's name.

The next day Judy and Mildred appeared at Wilkerson's office. Wilkerson had a short discussion with them, convincing them that Judy stood a good chance of making it in movies, and then he ushered them over to see agent Henry Wilson.

Consequently, a little film work came her way. She was an extra in *A Star Is Born* for David O. Selznick, but no studio was interested in signing her to a contract. Finally she was called to an interview at Warner Bros., where director Mervyn LeRoy was looking for someone to play a teenage murder victim in *They Won't Forget*.

He gave her one word of command. 'Walk.'

She walked. She got the job.

He suggested that she change her name from Judy to Lana, and a contract with Warners was drawn up. She started at $50 a week, increasing to a final sum of $600 a week over seven years.

Lana's role in *They Won't Forget* lasted barely twelve minutes, yet is legendary. She had little more than eighteen lines of dialogue, but the highlight of her appearance was a 75-foot tracking shot of her walking down a street. She wore spiked-heel shoes, a tight skirt, a saucy beret and a tight sweater that hugged her mature figure so tantalizingly, that she provided the cinema with the most sizzling scene of that year.

And yet the whole sequence is tinged with irony. Beginning with Lana in school and shifting quickly to her drinking pop in a soda fountain, it was recreating the now legendary turning-point in her life. The scene ends with her murder, a crime which hit her own life twice; first when her father was killed and secondly when her own lover was stabbed to death.

Not surprisingly, Lana was dubbed 'The Sweater Girl', and a star was born.

Further bit parts followed and in 1940 she bleached her hair blonde, starred in *Ziegfeld Girl* and became one of the biggest stars at MGM where she was under contract. That same year, on 13 February, she married band leader Artie Shaw. Two months later the marriage was over and she suffered a nervous breakdown. They divorced that same year on 12 September.

Two years later she was enjoying time out at a Los Angeles nightclub. A young businessman, Stephen Crane, couldn't help but notice the famous and gorgeous star. For a bet he asked her to dance. Nine days later, on 17 July 1942, they were man and wife. But the marriage had to be quickly annulled. Crane's own divorce had not been finalized and he suddenly risked a charge of bigamy. They were remarried on 14 March 1943, by which time she was pregnant. Five months later little Cheryl was born, suffering from the Rhesus Negative factor, resulting in a series of blood transfusions.

But this marriage was also doomed and they were divorced in August 1944.

Lana couldn't help letting her heart rule her head. She married again in 1948 to millionaire Henry J. 'Bob' Topping. It lasted barely four years. By that time she was earning a salary of $5,000 a week at Metro and proved she was worth it by being sensational in an equally sensational movie, *The Bad and the Beautiful* in 1953.

That was the year in which she married screen Tarzan Lex Barker. Four years later they were divorced.

Lana was then in her mid-thirties, and by Hollywood

standards, that was almost past it. The poor films Metro were choosing for her were not helping her career. She even tried a new look by dyeing her hair dark, but in 1955 she was blonde again for the trashy so-called Biblical epic *The Prodigal.*

In a daring bid to give her career a lift, she left MGM and went freelance. It was a traumatic time for her, but Johnny Stompanato was just around the corner.

They called him Johnny Valentine. He must have thought he was Rudolph Valentino. He certainly had the Latin good looks, and he offered himself to rich widows who wanted company. He had a number of aquaintances in the film industry.

In the spring of 1957 he succeeded in acquiring Lana Turner's private phone number. He knew about her latest marriage break-up, and he figured he could ease her loneliness. He called her, mentioned the names of a few mutual friends, and suggested they meet for a blind date. She responded with her usual impulsiveness, and they got together. She seemed immediately smitten by him. She knew he had underground connections, and she wholeheartedly believed him when he told her he was five years older than she. In fact, he was five years younger.

It was certainly a difficult time for Lana. Her private life had hardly been a bed of roses, and her many problems had affected Cheryl. The girl spent much of her time either with her grandmother or at various expensive private schools. The continual change of step-fathers seemed to put a strain on the mother-daughter relationship and when Cheryl was away from her mother, she didn't waste ink writing too many letters home to Mom.

In April 1957, Cheryl ran away from school. In desperation she approached a strange man and begged him to help her to find a hotel room where she could hide, she said, from three men who were following her. She was fortunate enough to have accosted a decent man who, instead, took her straight to the police station. Cheryl admitted who she was and the police contacted Lana and Stephen Crane who both rushed to the station to collect their daughter.

Cheryl now began spending time with her mother and met

Johnny. She approved of the relationship because she seemed to recognize that her mother really was in love with him. And he was completely obsessed with Lana. The whole episode brought about a change in Cheryl. While at one particular school she had been told that she either wrote to her mother once a week or go to bed hungry. She began her first letter saying, 'Dear Mother, this is not a letter, it's a meal ticket.' But now she kept in touch constantly, and even wrote to Johnny.

'Give my love to Mother,' she wrote once. 'Write soon and be good. Love ya and miss ya loads, Cherie.'

In 1958 Lana and Johnny were separated for a while when she came to England to make *Another Time, Another Place* with Sean Connery. Lana's heart ached for her Johnny. She wrote to him constantly, referring to herself as 'Little Lana' and calling him 'Daddy' or 'Papite'. She still believed him to be older and tended to treat him as a father figure.

She told him, 'I adore the way you write and all the truly beautiful things you say to me – so, please, please dearest continue. Every line warms me and makes me ache and miss you more each tiny moment. It's true – it's beautiful yet terrible. But, just so is deep love . . . we certainly are in tune "all the way." . . . Know how dearly I love you angel . . . hold me dear lover mi macho.'

Finally, unable to bear to be apart from him any longer, Lana paid for his plane ticket and he came to her. They set up home in a huge house in London, but behind locked doors it was not all passion. There was a jealous and violent streak that ran straight through him which he couldn't shake off. She had allowed him to dominate her, but he began to exert a dominion that was frightening.

'When I say "hop" you'll hop,' he commanded her. 'When I say "jump" you'll jump.'

At one time he threatened to really hurt her, and her fear of him grew. When he actually came to the film set waving a gun, Sean Connery warned him, 'Stay away from Lana.' A fight ensued and Connery decked him.

Still the threats were thrown at her. 'I'll mutilate you, I'll hurt you so you'll be so repulsive you'll have to hide for ever.' He even attempted to strangle her and threatened her with a razor blade.

The studio, concerned for the welfare of their star, called in Scotland Yard and Stompanato was ordered out of the country.

But Lana's love for her Valentine was stronger than her fear of him, and she continued to write to him. When the filming was over, they flew off to Acapulco for a holiday. They made so much noise with their passion in their hotel room that the other guests complained.

When they returned to Los Angeles in March Cheryl, now fourteen, tall and made up to look eighteen, was waiting. The following month Cheryl was at home with them for the Easter holidays. The week before the Easter weekend, she had gone with her mother to the Academy Awards ceremony. Lana had been nominated Best Actress for *Peyton Place*. She was pipped at the post by Susan Hayward for her performance in *I Want to Live*.

Although *Peyton Place* didn't give Lana the Oscar, it did bring about a new direction in her career which, for some years, had been faltering. For the first time, Lana appeared on screen as a mother who was past her youth and searching for love and happiness. It seemed to echo the real Lana Turner.

Still devoted to her father, Cheryl spent much of Good Friday with him. At around half-past five she returned to her mother's house on North Bedford Drive. That evening she killed Johnny 'Valentine' Stompanato.

The phone in Jerry Geisler's house rang. He answered the call.

'This is Lana Turner,' said a distraught voice. 'Something terrible has happened. Could you please come to my house.'

Geisler, Hollywood's most famous and sought after attorney, wasted no time. He arrived at the Moorish house to find Lana in tears and daughter Cheryl near hysteria. On the floor of Lana's bedroom lay the body of Johnny Stompanato.

Geisler, who had in the past defended the likes of Errol Flynn, Charlie Chaplin and even Bugsy Siegel, now had the task of defending Lana Turner's teenage daughter Cheryl on a manslaughter charge.

But not everybody was prepared to believe that a young girl was responsible for the death of the small-time gangster and gigolo.

On the morning of 5 April, Sean Connery was awakened by the phone ringing in his Hollywood hotel room.

'If I were you, I'd get out of town fast,' advised the caller, explaining that Johnny Stompanato had been killed and certain of his friends were well aware of Connery's confrontation with Stompanato in England. Connery took the caller's advice, and before noon he had paid his bill and was gone from Los Angeles.

If any of Stompanato's friends did have any reason to suspect Sean Connery, the police certainly didn't share their theory. Cheryl Crane had admitted to killing her mother's lover, and as soon as this news was made public, Lana Turner's stormy love life once again became fodder for the newspapers.

Almost every American columnist slammed Lana as being a dissolute mother. Her love letters were published in the press and only Walter Winchell of all the powerful columnists sprang to her defence:

> She is made of rays of the sun, woven of blue eyes, honey-colored hair and flowing curves. She is Lana Turner, goddess of the screen. But soon, the magician leaves and the shadows take over. All the hidden cruelties appear. She is lashed by vicious reporting, flogged by editorials, and threatened with being deprived of her child. And of course, it is outraged virtue which screams the loudest. It seems sadistic to me to subject Lana to any more torment. No punishment that could be imagined could hurt her more than the memory of this nightmarish event. And she is condemned to live with this memory to the end of her days.
>
> In short, give your heart to the girl with the broken heart.

As Winchell had pointed out, much of America and the press put the blame for Stompanato's death squarely on the beautiful shoulders of Lana Turner. And in a real sense she, as well as Cheryl, was on trial when the inquest went out live on American television on 11 April. Not surprisingly, it proved to be the biggest show of the season.

Besides defending Cheryl, Geisler knew he had to publicly defend Lana as well. Calling each of them to the stand, he had them testify to the happenings of the evening of 4 April. For

Cheryl, just fourteen year of age, it was harrowing. For Lana, an experienced actress, it was her most terrifying appearance before an audience. And the whole of America was watching.

But through each emotional breakdown, through every near-faint, Jerry Geisler guided Lana and daughter in recreating the events that had led to Stompanato's death.

Cheryl had returned to her mother's home on Good Friday at five-thirty in the evening. She went straight to her room to watch TV. Suddenly her mother walked in, followed by Stompanato who was in a furious temper. He filled the room with his verbal abuse.

'I'll cut you up and I'll get your mother and your daughter too,' he screamed. 'That's my business.'

Lana rebuked him for saying 'such things' in front of Cheryl who sat back terrified. A little later, after Lana and Stompanato had left her room, she found her way to the kitchen and took a carving knife. She did this, she told the court 'in case he tried to hurt Mother'.

Shortly after, another furious argument broke out between Lana and Stompanato, this time in Lana's bedroom.

Lana testified, 'No matter what I did, how I tried to get away, he would never leave. And I would have to do everything he told me or he'd cut my face or cripple me. He would kill me, and my daughter and my mother.'

Cheryl then came into the room and Lana pleaded with her to leave and forget what she had heard. Cheryl hesitated for a moment, then obediently left.

It was not long before the voices were raised again with Stompanato still threatening Lana with violence. Cheryl had stood outside, hysteria rising within her at the sounds coming from her mother's room. Unable to stand it any longer, she burst in and saw Stompanato swinging at Lana with a jacket on a coat hanger.

Cheryl walked over to Stompanato.

Lana Turner told the court, 'Everything happened so quickly that I did not even see the knife in my daughter's hand. I thought she had hit him in the stomach with her fist. Mr

Stompanato stumbled forward, turned around and fell on his back. He choked, his hands on his throat. I ran to him and lifted up his sweater.

'I saw the blood – he made a horrible noise in his throat . . .'

America watched as Lana at this point broke down in tears, almost fainting. Geisler gently urged her on. She continued.

'I tried to breathe air into his semi-open lips . . . my mouth against his . . .'

She began to pass out and Geisler lifted her up. A bailiff brought her a glass of water.

In a choking voice, Lana finished her testimony: 'He was dying.'

While Stompanato had been in his final death throes, Lana had summoned her mother who immediately called for a doctor. While the doctor administered an adrenalin shot to Stompanato, Mrs Turner tried mouth-to-mouth resuscitation. But Stompanato's heart stopped. The doctor looked at Lana and suggested she call Jerry Geisler.

As the whole scene formed in the minds of every viewer and every member of the jury, a man suddenly leapt to his feet in court and shouted, 'This whole thing's a pack of lies! Johnny Stompanato was my friend. The daughter was in love with him, and he was killed because of jealousy between mother and daughter.'

But no one else believed they were witnessing anything other than a confused, frightened, weeping woman revealing every-thing, including the fact that she and Stompanato had begun quarrelling that evening because she had at last discovered his true age. All the time he had fostered the lie that he was five years older than she was. That he was actually five years younger than she was a revelation that had infuriated her, resulting in Stompanato's typical outburst of violence.

Following Lana Turner's testimony, it did not take the coroner's jury long to arrive at a verdict: justifiable homicide. Cheryl Crane was free to go.

Johnny Stompanato was buried in his home town in Illinois. Mickey Cohen paid for the funeral. Shortly after Stompanato's brother filed a suit for $800,000 damages against Lana Turner and Stephen Crane for alleged parental negligence. The matter was settled by Geisler out of court, and Stompanato's bereaved family received a settlement of some $20,000.

As for Lana's career, judging by past movie scandals, it might have been expected that Miss Turner would have promptly retired from the screen. But she followed the trial with her biggest box-office hit ever, *Imitation of Life*. It virtually put the ailing Universal Studios back on their feet and earned for its star 50 per cent of the picture's profits. With her money, she set up a trust fund that ensured that she would receive an income for life.

She also continued to get married, and remarried. Her husband from November 1960 to October 1962 was rancher Fred May. Next came businessman Robert Eaton from June 1965 to April 1969. She then married Ronald Dante, a hypnotist, in May 1969 but they were separated six months later and divorced in 1972.

As for Cheryl, she grew up to follow in her father's footsteps in the running of a chain of restaurants in Los Angeles.

Today the death of Johnny Stompanato is something neither mother nor daughter ever discusses. It marks the blackest moment of both lives, but it also had one very positive effect. It finally brought mother and daughter together in a relationship that looks like enduring, having gone through fourteen years of separation with confusion and frustration for Cheryl.

But, as Lana Turner says, 'When two human beings go through a tremendous emotional experience as we did, it either cracks them apart or brings them closer together. Cheryl and I became closer.'

Murder at the Alamo

HE WORE COWBOY boots and buckskins. The wide-brimmed
hat shaded his face from the bright sun. He stood six-feet-four,
even without the boots. He walked with the air and authority of
a pioneer leader as he strode across the rugged ground of
Bracketville in Texas.

But this was not the old West: it was October 1959, and the
big man with the ten-gallon hat was John Wayne. It may have
all been pretend, but his commanding personality was authentic.
He was a man in control and in charge.

Around him hundreds of men and women, most of them
arrayed in the classic Western garb of the 1830s, mingled
around trucks and wiring and huge arc lamps and cameras. The
film they were making was the realization of a dream for the
man they called Duke.

For many years he had planned and plotted and schemed and
virtually sold his soul to bring to the screen the momentous
events of 1836 when 185 Texans and Kentuckians held back the
7,000 troops of the Mexican dictator General Santa Anna at the
broken-down mission-turned-fortress, the Alamo.

Wayne not only starred as Davy Crockett, but he was
personally producing and directing the great American epic as
well. Some $8,000,000 were riding on this movie, much of it
from Wayne's own personal resources. *The Alamo* was a picture
he had to make and, come hell or high water, he would make it
at whatever cost, especially to himself.

He had enlisted the elite of Hollywood, both in front of and
behind the cameras. The brilliant English actor Laurence
Harvey was portraying William Travis, Richard Widmark was
the legendary Jim Bowie, Richard Boone was portraying Sam
Houston and hundreds of others had supporting roles and walk-
on parts, and thousands of extras had been recruited for the
awesome battle scenes. Art director Alfred Ybarra had recon-
structed in exact detail the Alamo as it had looked in 1836, and

Cliff Lyons was responsible for directing the breath-taking action and battle sequences.

The film had been two years in production, and Wayne was hanging just about everything he had on this one picture. He could not afford to let anything interfere with filming.

Suddenly a horseman rode over the horizon, going hell-for-leather like a Pony Express rider. He'd ridden many miles over the rugged landscape towards this remote location. He pulled up hard as he reached Wayne and leapt from his saddle. He had the gravest news to give to his boss, the Duke. One of his featured actresses, LaJean Ethridge, had been murdered. The sheriff who had been called to the scene of the crime had said that it was an open and shut case.

'Her boyfriend was jealous,' the sheriff had announced, 'and he thought he would lose her. So he stabbed her with a knife. It's as simple as that.'

But that was little comfort to Wayne. As much as he mourned the loss of a girl he had liked, he also foresaw disaster if he allowed her murder to get in the way of the film's progress. There was nothing for it but to carry on with the filming regardless.

But, as the biggest Hollywood star of them all was to discover, neither he nor his multi-million-dollar epic could remain untouched or unaffected by murder.

Fifteen hours earlier, LaJean Ethridge had begun to see her dreams of stardom coming to fruition as she returned to the bunkhouse where she was staying in Spofford. Suddenly she was no longer just a bit player threatened with being swamped in a deluge of a cast of thousands and going virtually unnoticed, but a featured actress in a major supporting role.

Her promotion from having just one line and a weekly fee of $75 to speaking whole passages of dialogue and a raise to $350 a week meant that she had to be closer to the film set, to rehearse more and be ready to be called at a moment's notice.

She was moving down to Bracketville to the sprawling Shehan Ranch where Wayne, Widmark, Harvey and the rest of the main cast were staying.

She was packing her things in her room when in walked Chester Harvey Smith. Chet, as he was known, was a lean, hungry-looking character with a wisp of a beard. He, LaJean and four other men were a company of touring actors who had all been assigned bit parts in *The Alamo*. They all shared this bunkhouse, and naturally Chet was surprised to see LaJean packing.

She was not exquisitely beautiful. She did not have the looks that would have made her a sex-symbol. But behind her twenty-seven-year-old face seemed to be the soul of a woman with a hundred years of experience; the kind of woman who once crossed the plains in a covered wagon; who watched her menfolk die in battle; who helped to settle the farthermost regions of the old American West. Her eyes seemed to reflect sad memories and her long face, accented by a jutting chin, just cried out to belong to a character actress. And now, after years of playing small towns with her five fellow-actors, she was at last to be given a stab at screen stardom.

Wayne's associate, Jim Heneghan, explained: 'I saw LaJean and Smith acting with a touring company. We engaged her for a one-line part but she impressed us so much that we gave her a full page of dialogue. She was one of the most talented actresses I've seen, and Wayne was so pleased with her that he asked the Screen Actors' Guild to enrol her as a member.'

And now it seemed that LaJean was deserting, not so much their little company, but Smith. At least, that's how Chet saw it, because he loved her. She loved him, too, but the prospect of passing up an opportunity like this was unthinkable.

'Where are you going?' he asked her moodily.

'To Bracketville,' she said excitedly, and explained to him about her big break. But he didn't have the same look of expectancy that she displayed.

'You're not going,' he suddenly yelled, and then threw himself on to a couch in another room, his jealousy building up inside him like steam in an engine.

She continued packing, and when finished she came out of her room, her suitcase in her hand. Smith leapt at her as she headed for the door. He grabbed her wrist and for a few moments she struggled against him.

Suddenly there was a Bowie knife in his hand – similar to the one used by Widmark in the film – and he drove it into her breast. She slumped to the floor and he cradled her in his arms. The horror of what he'd done pierced him. She moaned her final words. 'I love you.' And then she died.

He was found cradling her dead body by Ray Henschell, one of the touring actors. Chet looked up at him and said sobbing, 'I don't care what happens to me now. My whole life is gone now she is dead.'

Henschell called for the sheriff who quickly arrived with a number of deputies like a veritable posse. But Smith offered no resistance at all.

'I couldn't stand being without her,' he told them as they led him away.

There really was nothing much to prove. Smith had admitted killing LaJean. The examining trial that was held five days later in the tiny courthouse in Bracketville shouldn't have caused any great stir.

But it did. Something was going on, and it seemed to revolve around John Wayne.

He had not been a witness to the killing. He'd been nowhere near the place when Smith killed LaJean. But Smith's lawyer from San Antonio, Fred Samaan, wanted Wayne on the witness stand. Samaan was unhappy about the way the whole case was being handled. It seemed as though District Attorney Douglas A. Newton was intent on getting this case to court and out again as quickly as possible.

Samaan's interests, of course, were with his client, who had confessed to the crime. And Samaan thought he smelled a rat, and wondered whether Wayne was involved.

Smith's lawyer served Wayne with a subpoena to appear in court. The next thing Samaan knew, Wayne was calling him on the phone, his gravel voice drawling, 'Listen, Mr Samaan, I ain't coming.'

'Then by God, Mr Wayne, I'll have you thrown in jail,' warned Samaan.

When news got around that Wayne was to be on the witness

stand and that something was stirring, reporters and TV newsmen from all over the country converged on the old Bracketville courthouse, expecting to see for themselves what all the fuss was about. And the very fact that Wayne was in court giving testimony concerning a murder was news itself.

But they were all to be disappointed. District Attorney Newton gave Justice of the Peace Albert Postel clear instructions: the hearing was to be closed to the public and the press. No reason for this decision was given, and a cloud of mystery descended on the whole episode.

Wayne's own attorney arrived with him and immediately issued a protest. States Attorney Leon Douglas went so far as to warn Postel that such a closed hearing might actually be contrary to state law. But Postel was adamant. Nobody knew then that he was merely acting upon the orders of the DA.

Nobody was happy about the closed doors. Samaan voiced his disapproval, convinced somebody was up to something, and just because Wayne's own attorney had protested as well was not enough to convince Samaan that Wayne was not behind it. In fact, he had his own suspicions about Wayne which was why he had called him to the hearing in the first place.

Very little about the trial is known today. The newsmen who were there recorded only what they saw from outside. First to go in was Art Names, one of the members of the touring company to which Smith and LaJean belonged. He went in at 9.30 a.m. and didn't emerge again until almost noon.

That was when big John Wayne came on the scene. He took the witness stand, but no one, except those inside and involved in the case, ever knew exactly what he had said.

When he came out a little later, the reporters swarmed round him. He retained his usual good humour and said, 'Sorry fellers, but I'm bound by the court's order not to reveal what I said.'

Later, when the hearing was over, Kinney County Prosecutor John Tobin was ordered by Postel to give a brief statement to the press to try and placate their curiosity over the closed-doors hearing and suppress any further mystery. Tobin told the gathered newsmen that Justice of the Peace Albert Postel had taken full responsibility for closing the hearing to outsiders, and had done it 'because of the intimate testimony given by Mr

Wayne and the four men who lived in the same house as Miss Ethridge'.

Such a statement, with the words, 'intimate testimony' did little more than arouse everybody's suspicions and curiosity even more. When certain reporters tried to approach the DA himself over the matter, all Newton would say was, 'I'm not saying anything. I have my reasons.'

Since then, the 'intimate testimony' of John Wayne has never been made public and its bearing on the case has therefore remained uncertain. It didn't take long for people to start possible theories, though. One question that everyone wanted to know was, just exactly where in Bracketville was LaJean going to be living?

The rumourmongers, of course, came up with possible answers, and they all pointed to John Wayne and his reputation as a ladies' man. It was true that Wayne had been greatly impressed with LaJean as an actress. Could he have also taken an interest in her in a more private way? And was it really so necessary for LaJean to move in with the big names in Bracketville?

Why should Chester Smith be suddenly overcome with such jealousy when, after all, there were four other men living under the same roof with them?

It cannot be overlooked, in trying to answer these questions sensibly, that LaJean was not a beautiful woman. Wayne had always favoured beautiful women. What's more, his three wives had all been of Latin extraction. LaJean was pale and blonde. She was not Wayne's type at all and, being who he was, he could have had any woman he wanted, for there have always been aspiring young actresses since the movies began who would do just about anything for a start in life.

All this, of course, does nothing to clear up the mystery, but simply adds to it. The fact remains that not enough is known about the trial.

However, it is known that Wayne had not wanted to attend the hearing, and came only when threatened with arrest. Smith's lawyer, Samaan, had suspected something was wrong, and he wanted Wayne to take the stand and let the court know that because of LaJean's death, many scenes would have to be reshot at great expense. Samaan strongly believed that Wayne was responsible for getting the DA to push this case faster than was necessary.

Whether or not this was proven from Wayne's 'intimate testimony' is still an enigma. But it is true that he wanted to get on with filming. After all, this motion picture was for him the dream of a lifetime come true.

From its beginnings the production had been plagued with problems. Several years earlier Wayne had begun work on the picture in Mexico, but was forced to abandon filming after just a month because already it was over-shooting the budget. Finally, in October 1957, Wayne began filming *The Alamo*, expecting it to cost around $8,000,000. It eventually rose to $12,000,000, and Wayne was up to his neck in debt.

Not surprisingly, then, Wayne was apprehensive about taking time off to make a court appearance that, in direct connection with the murder, was of no value at all. But could it also be true that Wayne had succeeded in putting pressure on the DA to hurry the case along? If so, then Wayne must have been in direct violation of the law for even attempting to interfere with the hearing. And the DA, aware of his own willingness to be so coerced, would certainly have had reason enough to close the doors of the court on the press, especially with Samaan so intent on bringing these facts out in court.

If all this is true, it must certainly be said that there are many others who have done more vile things to corrupt justice. But it does perhaps show that such big-name stars as John Wayne could still, when necessary, have an influence over those to whom we entrust the enforcing of the law.

Whatever the truth of that, it had no real bearing on the actual case. Chester Smith didn't so much as make a pitiful attempt to throw himself on the court's mercy. It was as though he wanted to pay for his crime, and he was sentenced to thirty years in prison.

After serving less than eight years, Chester Harvey Smith was paroled.

CASE 8

Los Angeles Police File: 'Marilyn Monroe – Murder'

SERGEANT JACK CLEMMONS had had all kinds of nutty calls come through to him over the years whenever he was on the desk as watch commander at the West Los Angeles police station. But never before had one been as bizarre if false or as historically tragic if true as the one that had come through to him at 4.25 a.m., Sunday 5 August 1962 from some doctor saying that Marilyn Monroe was dead. It was possible, thought Sergeant Clemmons, that this was just a gag.

That was why he went himself straight to the Beverly Hills home where resided the Hollywood actress who was not only one of the greatest movie stars of all time, but just about the most desirable woman in the world. No other woman in the history of the cinema – not even Jean Harlow – had ever embodied so fully the overworked publicity tag, 'sex symbol'.

Considering that Monroe was something of a legend in her own lifetime, Sergeant Clemmons may well have been surprised to find on his arrival that Monroe's home was relatively modest by Hollywood standards. But what surprised him more than anything else was the number of people who were there, even before the police had been called. He 'thought it looked like a convention'.

Besides Monroe's housekeeper Mrs Eunice Murray, there was Marilyn's psychiatrist Dr Ralph Greenson, her own practitioner Dr Hyman Engelberg, her press agent Pat Newcomb, Mrs Inez Melson who was legal guardian of Marilyn's mentally ill mother, and Mrs Murray's son-in-law who worked as Marilyn's gardener.

In the master bedroom, Clemmons found Marilyn lying dead in bed. He had gone because he 'wanted to make sure I was not having a joke pulled on us'. He knew now it was no gag. Monroe was dead, probably from an overdose of barbiturates.

He began asking questions. Mrs Murray told him she had become alarmed about Marilyn round about midnight and had called Dr Greenson. Dr Greenson had told her to try the bedroom door and then the window while he held on the line. Mrs Murray couldn't get through the bedroom door but had managed to see in through the window. When she reported to Dr Greenson that Marilyn was just lying on the bed, he came straight over, broke in through the window and finally opened up the bedroom door. He told Mrs Murray, 'We've lost her. *Rigor mortis* has already set in.'

Dr Engelberg arrived shortly after and confirmed that Monroe was dead. That was the story they gave. But Sergeant Clemmons was mystified about something. He asked the doctors how soon they had arrived following Mrs Murray's discovery of Marilyn at midnight.

They both told him that they were there within half an hour.

Then why, he asked, had they not called the police station for almost four hours? Sergeant Clemmons says, 'One of the doctors gave me an answer that didn't make any sense. There was no adequate explanation for that delay.'

Sergeant Clemmons became even more suspicious over the doctors' conclusion that Marilyn had probably died from an overdose of barbiturates. He looked at Marilyn's body laying face down, almost peacefully. It appeared to him 'that the scene had been arranged'. He noticed that

her legs were parallel, and she looked just what she was – a dead body that had been put into that position. When she died, she would not have been in that position. There is no possibility of a person dying of an overdose that way. In deaths from barbiturates, in the last moments before con-sciousness is lost, there is pain and there's contortion. It's common to find the body twisted. You never see a body with the legs straight. And I've seen many hundreds of suicides by drug overdose.

That was Sergeant Clemmons's observation, and in his mind he had no doubt that 'somebody murdered her. Obviously it wasn't a suicide, anybody could see that.'

But Sergeant Clemmons didn't have the chance to follow up on his theory. When the detectives arrived on the scene, he returned to the police station and was astounded when he learned that there was to be no murder inquiry. The decision had been taken by the Police Chief, William Parker, to order a suicide verdict, and so it was that on the morning of Sunday 5 August, the news was heard on radio, 'Marilyn Monroe is dead, apparently from an overdose of sleeping pills.'

Clemmons could hardly believe it. He just knew there was a whole lot wrong, and later that morning his conviction was made all the stronger when one of the investigating detectives, Sergeant R.E. Byron, made out his official report. It read:

Marilyn Monroe, on August 4, 1962, retired to her bedroom at about eight o'clock in the evening; Mrs Eunice Murray noted a light in Miss Monroe's bedroom. Mrs Murray was not able to arouse Miss Monroe when she went to the door, and when she tried the door again at 3.30 a.m., when she noted the light still on, she found it to be locked. Thereupon Mrs Murray observed Miss Monroe through the bedroom window and found her lying on her stomach in the bed and the appearance seemed unnatural.

Mrs Murray then called Miss Monroe's pyschiatrist, Dr Ralph Greenson. Upon entering after breaking the bedroom window, he found Miss Monroe possibly dead. Then he telephoned Dr Hyman Engelberg, who came over and then pronounced Miss Monroe dead at 3.35 a.m.

Miss Monroe was seen by Dr Greenson on August 4, 1962 at 5.15 p.m., at her request, because she was not able to sleep. She was being treated by him for about a year.

She was nude when Dr Greenson found her dead with the telephone receiver in one hand and lying on her stomach. The police department was called and when they arrived, they found Miss Monroe in the condition described above, except for the telephone which was removed by Dr Greenson.

There were found to be 15 bottles of medication on the night table and some were prescription. A bottle marked $1\frac{1}{2}$ grains Nembutal, prescription 20853 and prescribed by Dr Engelberg, and referring to this particular bottle, Dr Engelberg made the statement that he prescribed a refill for this about two days ago and he further stated there probably should have been 50 capsules at the time this was refilled by the pharmacist.

Description of Deceased: Female Caucasian, age 36, height 5'4", weight 115 pounds, blonde hair, blue eyes, and slender, medium build.

Occupation: Actress. Probable cause of death: overdose of Nembutal, body discovered 8/5/62 [5 August, 1962] at 3.35 a.m. Taken to County Morgue – from there to Westwood Mortuary.

There was no doubt in Sergeant Clemmons's mind. When he had arrived at Monroe's house Mrs Murray and the two doctors had all agreed that it had been about midnight when Mrs Murray called them. Now their stories had changed and they had some holes in them. According to the report, Mrs Murray had seen Marilyn's body through the bedroom window *before* she called Dr Greenson, and that the time was not midnight but 3.30 a.m. Then Dr Greenson managed to arrive on the scene, examine Monroe's body, call Dr Engelberg who arrived there and pronounced Miss Monroe dead at 3.35 a.m., all in *five minutes*.

Not too surprisingly, Detective Sergeant Byron was ordered to question the doctors again the following day. Byron reported, 'Both agree to the following time sequence of their actions,' and went on to note that Dr Greenson had received the call from Mrs Murray 'at 3.30 a.m., stating that she was unable to get into Miss Monroe's bedroom and the light was on.' Byron reported that Dr Greenson then told Mrs Murray to 'pound on the door and look in the window and call him back'. Now the time switches to 3.35 a.m. when 'Mrs Murray called back' reporting on what she saw through the window. Dr Greenson, now dressed, left for Monroe's house which, Byron noted, was 'about one mile away'. Byron adds that Dr Greenson told Mrs Murray to call Dr Engelberg.

Dr Greenson's time of arrival is now put down at 3.40 a.m. He entered the window and examined her. '*Rigor mortis* had set in. At 3.50 a.m. Dr Engelberg arrived and pronounced Miss Monroe dead.' Byron goes on to say that both doctors believe it was about 4.00 a.m. when Dr Engelberg called the police.

As far as Police Chief Parker was concerned, that story tied matters up nicely. The times were more realistic and everything was straightforward. But still Sergeant Clemmons was not satisfied. For a start, apart from the times, the two reports given within twenty-four hours of each other were contradictory regarding whether or not Mrs Murray called Dr Greenson before or after she saw Monroe lying lifeless on the bed, as well as concerning who exactly called Dr Engelberg. And what still didn't add up was the doctors' 'belief' that they called the police station at 4.00. Clemmons knew it was 4.25. *He* was the one who took the call.

Something was wrong – he could smell it – and he began to insist that Police Chief Parker order a murder investigation. Clemmons was told bluntly to keep quiet. He refused and was dropped from the force.

Police Chief William Parker was a very powerful and ambitious man entrusted with keeping the law. He alone had the authority to order a suicide verdict, and no one but a coroner could reverse that verdict. Parker assured everyone that all the circumstances of Marilyn's death pointed to a suicide very strongly.

It was therefore a rather irrational and pointless move when Parker seized from the telephone company the records itemizing all of Monroe's long-distance and local phone calls for July and August. Parker didn't even attempt to keep that action secret and showed it to a number of newspaper reporters. To columnist Florabel Muir he made the peculiar boast that the phone record was his guarantee of getting the FBI directorship 'when Bobby became President'. He was talking of Bobby Kennedy who, according to Parker, had confided in him that he was planning to fire Edgar Hoover as head of the FBI and that Parker had a good chance of succeeding Hoover. Parker also told Muir that the telephone record showed that Marilyn had made several calls during July to Bobby Kennedy.

To James Hudson, the United Press International news editor, Parker revealed that 'at least six phone calls' had been made from Marilyn's home to the Justice Department in the past month. And to newscaster George Putnam, Parker said,

'Marilyn was trying to reach Mr Kennedy. She called the Justice Department in Washington, DC. Not his private number but through the switchboard. Marilyn tried to reach Bobby Kennedy on eight different occasions the weeks before she died but was unsuccessful.'

It seemed that on the one hand Parker had made an attempt to protect Bobby Kennedy by seizing the phone records, yet on the other he was openly revealing that there was some connection between Marilyn Monroe and Bobby Kennedy. But these were the pre-Watergate days when no columnist or newscaster, no matter how powerful, dared to publish anything remotely scandalous about such powerful political figures, especially a man like Bobby Kennedy who was not only a senator, not only the Attorney General, but the brother of the President of the United States.

For years following Monroe's death, rumours circulated wildly about an affair between Marilyn and Bobby Kennedy, as well as one between Marilyn and President John Kennedy. Today the evidence is undeniable that Monroe did indeed have romantic involvements with the Kennedy brothers, but even up to ten years ago the general public thought the rumours unfounded, and those who were in the know were reluctant to reveal all.

Today one thing is absolutely certain; every effort was made in the hours and days following Marilyn Monroe's death to keep Bobby Kennedy's name completely out of the picture. Police Chief Parker's seizure of the telephone records was just a small part of this effort, as will be seen. Parker's big mistake was in confiding in professional journalists who would, at some time in the future when the press was more free to speak its mind in the post-Watergate era, spill the beans.

But even if Parker had kept quiet, the truth would still have surfaced. Truth has a knack of breaking through even the toughest barriers, no matter how long it takes. As far as Monroe's affairs with Bobby and John Kennedy were concerned, there were already too many people who knew about them and who would eventually talk.

Had it all taken place in the years following Watergate, columnist Sidney Skolsky would have had a story to tell. But when John F. Kennedy was President of the United States, no newspaper dared to print anything that would compromise the President in any way. Certainly Skolsky was not, in 1962, a man who wanted to make history by breaking the golden rule.

He was, in the years preceding Monroe's death, one of the few columnists who could claim to have been a friend of the blonde bombshell. Not surprisingly, in the spring of 1962 she confided to him that she was having an affair with one of the most powerful men in the world, and certainly the most powerful in America – President Kennedy. But it wasn't a story he could use, not for many years. And when he did, Marilyn Monroe was long dead. And so was John Kennedy. In retrospect, Skolsky says, 'I still find it grim to speculate what might have happened to me if I had tried to write about this affair in my column when it first came to my attention in 1962.'

Earl Wilson was another columnist with a story to tell, but like Sidney Skolsky, he didn't for years until he felt it was safe to. The story he wrote was one told to him by a man who claimed to be one of President Kennedy's 'beards' – that is, a man who publicly escorts a woman on a date to hide the fact that she is actually dating somebody else.

This particular 'beard' had to pick Marilyn up at her New York apartment and escort her to a special dinner party thrown by Kennedy at the Carlyle Hotel. They had to be there by 9 p.m. At 8.45 when the 'beard' arrived at the apartment, Marilyn was still asleep and undressed. The 'beard' ordered her to get dressed, and he picked a dress at random from her wardrobe and threw it at her. 'Put this on,' he shouted. He was scared to death of keeping the President waiting. But she still took her time, insisting on disguising herself and spending the next hour and a half looking for clothes and a dark wig.

Panic striken, the 'beard' begged her to hurry up. He went white when the phone rang and an angry voice demanded, 'Where is she?'

Finally, she was ready to go. The 'beard' led her to the waiting limousine, vowing, 'This is the last time. This is too much. Jack will kill me.'

Marilyn was calm and collected and tried to cool him down. When they arrived at the hotel, Kennedy was furious. But then he took one look at Marilyn in her tight, white dress, and he smiled. No more was said of her tardiness.

According to Sidney Skolsky, Marilyn told him that whenever John Kennedy was in Los Angeles, she met with him secretly at the beach home on Ocean Front of Peter and Pat Lawford. Pat was Kennedy's sister. Marilyn told Skolsky how difficult it was to maintain any privacy because the Secret Service was always outside, and if any lights went off, agents were likely to burst in.

Although her affair with the Prez, as she called him, had to be kept secret from the public, she made no effort to keep it secret from those close to her. She once told her masseur, Ralph Roberts, that she had dated Kennedy. It was well known at the time that Kennedy suffered from a bad back. When Roberts asked Marilyn how the date had gone, she replied, 'I think I made his back feel better.'

It had become an open secret in Hollywood, but no one dared speak of it publicly, especially Peter Lawford, the President's brother-in-law. In the years that followed Monroe's death, Lawford publicly denied any involvement between either Marilyn and John Kennedy, or Marilyn and Bobby Kennedy. The only person he ever confided in was Deborah Gould whom he married in 1971 following his divorce from Pat, but apart from that, Lawford's lips were sealed on the subject right up to his death. Today, Deborah Gould is able to reveal what Lawford had told her. Previously, all the stories of Monroe's affairs with the Kennedy brothers had remained rumours. But Deborah Gould confirms that the rumours are true. Monroe had 'a sexual relationship' with Bobby Kennedy, and, according to Miss Gould, it was 'much deeper than that'. In fact, Marilyn's affair with Bobby was a lot deeper and longer lasting than her fling with John. But if Peter and Pat Lawford ever thought that the secret rendezvous at their house would remain their private knowledge, they were terribly wrong.

As early as 1957 Bobby Kennedy had been taking Marilyn to the Desert Inn in Las Vegas, according to the hotel's manager Wilbur Clarke. The only reason he ever revealed that was because a friend of his wanted to know all about Kennedy's goings-on. That person was Jimmy Hoffa, the head of the Teamsters, America's Transport Union. Hoffa and Bobby Kennedy had a vendetta against each other. Bobby Kennedy had become obsessed with flushing out America's underworld, and he believed that Hoffa was hired by the mafia. During the late Fifties, Bobby Kennedy was involved in interrogating a number of people with possible mob links, including Hoffa. Bobby was intent on destroying Hoffa, and Hoffa was intent on revenge. He knew that any evidence of sexual indiscretion by either of the Kennedy brothers would destroy their political aspirations. When John Kennedy was inaugurated as President of the United States in 1961, Hoffa's espionage activities increased.

In the summer of 1961 Hoffa held a secret meeting in Florida to outline his plans to wreck John Kennedy's clean-cut image and ensure that his younger brother didn't succeed him in the Presidency. Private Investigator Fred Otash has revealed how he was summoned to that meeting where he was told by Hoffa that he wanted Peter Lawford's beach house at 625 Ocean Front bugged. Hoffa had hired bugging specialist Bernie Spindel. Otash and his men were to assist Spindel in recording the happenings within Lawford's home. Their task was to produce a devastating profile of the Kennedys, and their relationships with Monroe or any other women.

According to Otash, they put bugs under carpets, inside chandeliers, in ceiling fixtures, 'everywhere!' By November 1961 Otash and his men were listening in on Lawford's private parties. They clearly heard the voices of Marilyn and John Kennedy, according to one of the private investigators working for Otash. They would listen to footsteps leaving the living room and entering the bedroom where another transmitter would pick up the voices of Marilyn and the President alone, followed by the rustle of clothes being removed and the sound of the bedsprings squeaking.

When Marilyn's affair with John came to a close, she took up again with Bobby who also began showing up at Lawford's house and even came to her home. Her neighbour and friend Jeanne Carmen was actually there one day when Bobby arrived. He and Marilyn began kissing and cuddling, and Miss Carmen knew it was time for her to leave.

Like others who knew of Monroe's involvement with the Kennedys, Jeanne Carmen kept quiet for many years. But as the evidence has amassed so that there can be no denial of the affairs and little doubt of a cover-up over Marilyn's death, she, like others, has talked openly.

Marilyn's dallyings with the Kennedys seem to have been happy times for her. Certainly at that time in her life, happy times had become ever rarer. She suffered from depression and was as emotionally unstable as she was beautiful. Her private life was a mess, and she was beginning to fall apart in her work.

Her mother, Gladys Pearl Baker, had a long history of mental illness and a number of her family had committed suicide. Gladys was unmarried when Marilyn was born as Norma Jean Baker on 1 June 1926 in Los Angeles. Marilyn did not know who her father was until she was sixteen when she discovered her birth certificate and saw the name of her father – Edward Mortenson. He had been killed in a motorcycle accident when she was three. Throughout her childhood, Marilyn lived with various foster parents; she was neglected and, on one occasion, raped. At sixteen she was married to a young aircraft plant worker. The marriage was a disaster and a year later she tried to kill herself. She was divorced in 1946 by which time she had been discovered by an Army photographer who persuaded her to pose for pin-up pictures for the boys in uniform. Her pictures soon began appearing on magazine covers all over the country and inevitably Hollywood took an interest in her. She was signed up by Twentieth Century-Fox in August 1946, playing bit parts, and then working her way up through a succession of dumb platinum blonde roles. Then, in 1952, the legendary nude calendar photo of her was discovered, as well as the fact that her mother was in a mental institution. She weathered the storm and by 1954 she was Fox's biggest box-office attraction and was well on the way to becoming America's most popular sex symbol.

She married baseball star Joe DiMaggio in January 1954 but nine months later, while filming *The Seven Year Itch*, they were divorced. Upon completion of the film, she went to New York where she trained under Lee and Paula Strasberg at their prestigious Actors Studio. It was in New York that she met playwright Arthur Miller whom she married in June 1956.

Having emerged from the Actors Studio, Monroe took on a new image of 'star temperament' and erratic behaviour on the set. While filming *Some Like It Hot* in 1959 she constantly turned up late for work while her co-stars, Jack Lemmon and Tony Curtis, sat around for hours dressed in the tight skirts and high heels they wore for the film. It led to conflict between Curtis and Monroe, and it didn't help when Monroe's terrible insecurity began shining through when she kept forgetting her lines. Director Billy Wilder told Lemmon and Curtis, 'You'd better be good in every take because when she gets it right, that's the one we're gonna print.'

Sometimes it took up to forty takes just for Marilyn to get a single line of dialogue right. Finally Wilder resorted to taping her lines to the furniture on the set, hidden from the camera.

Paula Strasberg was constantly on the set at Monroe's insistence, and instead of going to Wilder for direction, Marilyn went to Strasberg.

When someone one day asked Wilder why he put up with Monroe, Wilder replied, 'I could get my auntie and she'd come to work on time and maybe even remember her lines. But the public wouldn't pay to see my auntie.'

He was right, on the screen Monroe was magic, but this belied the emotional torment she was going through. Things got so bad that shortly after the premiere of her last completed film, *The Misfits* in 1961, she was signed into Payne Whitney clinic, a psychiatric hospital in New York. Just a week earlier, on 21 January 1961, she had divorced Miller.

She was beset with emotional problems. Throughout the making of *The Misfits* she had continued to come late to the set each day. Often she didn't turn up at all due to one illness or another, and once she collapsed on the set from an overdose of sleeping pills and was rushed to hospital. She had become dependent on sleeping pills and alcohol, and a stay in Payne Whitney seemed the best hope of her keeping hold of her sanity. But once inside she became desperate to escape. She wrote to Lee Strasberg, begging. 'I'm locked up with all these poor nutty people. I'm sure to end up a nut if I stay in this nightmare. Please help me.'

It was Joe DiMaggio who came and obtained her release. Despite their divorce, they were still close friends and he cared very much for her. In fact, when he heard about her affair with Bobby Kennedy he reportedly quit his $100,000 a year job as vice-president of a business corporation to rush to her to warn her about Bobby, telling her that he was a known 'manipulator'. But his good intentions caused a tremendous row and he left. Afterwards she was sorry for arguing with him, and wrote him a letter in which she apologized and said that she wished she could make him happy. She wanted always to make at least one person completely happy but had always failed. She told Joe in the letter that *he* was the one person she really wanted to make completely happy.

The letter was never sent. It was found in her desk shortly after her death.

Under the guidance of Dr Greenson, who was endeavouring to help Monroe lose her dependence upon sleeping pills, Marilyn was ready to go back to work, and in the spring of 1962 she began filming *Something's Got to Give* with Dean Martin at Twentieth Century-Fox.

But little had changed. Shortly before filming commenced, the producer, Henry Weinstein, had rescued her from an overdose of barbiturates. She was still paranoid, still given to falling ill, still turning up late. The crew began to grow intolerant and the assistant director was heard to say, 'She makes Lucretia Borgia look like a pussycat.'

But Dean Martin, who was a close friend, seemed to understand and support her. When the studio threatened to fire her because she had failed to turn up yet again claiming she had flu, Martin saved her by announcing he too had flu and wouldn't be working for a day or two.

Weinstein also did his best to keep her on the film, but his patience began to run out when she asked if she could have time off on 18 and 19 May because, she said, her period was due then. Weinstein, however, had read in a newspaper that she had been invited to attend a gala birthday party for President Kennedy on 19 May.

'You can go to the President's birthday party with your period?' he yelled at her. 'What kind of period is that?'

'It's not really my period,' she replied. 'I just told you that to get off to go to the birthday party.'

As Weinstein said, 'I was furious, but what could I do?'

The huge party was held in Madison Square Garden and was attended by twenty thousand guests. It was a three-hour spectacle featuring celebrities such as Ella Fitzgerald, Harry Belafonte and Jack Benny. Toward the end of the show Peter Lawford stepped on the stage and announced, 'Mr President, ladies and gentlemen – Marilyn Monroe.'

There was rapturous applause, but no Monroe stepped into the spotlight. It was, in fact, something of a gag. Lawford called her name again. She still didn't show and the audience giggled nervously, unsure of how deliberate it all was. Finally, he said, 'Here she is, Mr President – the *late* Marilyn Monroe.'

She stepped into the spotlight, her body virtually exposed through her breathtaking, tight-fitting, flesh-coloured, silk dress. Then through pursed lips she sang the sexiest ever version of 'Happy Birthday to You' while a giant cake, complete with 41 candles, was wheeled out. Then the President took the stand and said, 'I can now retire from politics after having had "Happy Birthday" sung to me by such a sweet wholesome girl as Marilyn Monroe.'

The audience roared with laughter. Very few of them knew how much more there had once been between their President and their favourite movie siren.

Meanwhile, work on *Something's Got to Give* continued painstakingly slowly. Out of 35 days shooting, Marilyn turned up for only twelve. Finally the studio ran out of patience and on 8 June, just seven days after she'd celebrated her thirty-sixth birthday, they fired her.

Out of work, Marilyn began haunting Coldwater Canyon Park to watch the children at play. For hours she'd just sit there and watch the kids. It had always been a sorrow in her life that she'd never had a child of her own. She felt desperately lonely and even resorted to making an anonymous call to a local radio station to speak of her misery and solitude. She felt she had no one to turn to. And then she thought of Robert Slatzer.

She'd known Bob Slatzer since 1946 when she was still a model. They had become friends and then lovers and, in 1952, even went through a marriage ceremony in Mexico. No records exist of the marriage because, according to Slatzer, they quickly changed their minds and had the documents destroyed before they could be filed, so the marriage was never made official. But they had remained close friends and she often confided in him.

Just three weeks before she died she went to the public phone booth in the park and called Bob Slatzer. She sounded frightened and begged him to meet her. He quickly drove to a street corner where they'd arranged to meet, picked her up and drove her to Point Dume on the Pacific Coast Highway north of Malibu. There they sat on the beach and Marilyn poured her heart out to him.

She told him that she had had to call from the public phone booth because she was convinced her own telephone was bugged. The story sounded quite irrational until she produced a little red diary she kept. She showed it to Slatzer. He was stunned by what he read. She had recorded many of the things that Bobby Kennedy had talked about to her – things which were top secret. She told Slatzer she kept the diary because Bobby got angry when she couldn't remember the things he had talked about, so she jotted them down to study them.

Included was an entry about 'Murder Inc.' According to Slatzer, Marilyn told him, 'I didn't quite understand what Bobby was saying. But I remember him telling me that he was powerful enough to have people taken care of if they got in his way.' She believed that Bobby had underworld killers in his employ who were reportedly assigned by secret elements of the CIA to perform 'dirty' jobs.

Slatzer says that another entry read, 'Bobby told me he was going to have Castro assassinated'. All this was thirteen years before it was revealed that at that time President Kennedy had given the go-ahead for the CIA to employ members of the American mafia to kill Fidel Castro. In return the mobsters were to get back the casinos they'd lost in the Cuban revolution. But in 1962 all this was dangerous information to have.

According to Slatzer, Marilyn told him, 'Bobby told me that Jack let him handle the whole thing. He said he ran the country that day because Jack had taken medication for his back and wasn't feeling well.'

Another entry, according to Slatzer, read, 'Bobby told me, "I want to put that son of a bitch Jimmy Hoffa into jail, no matter how I do it." '

Now Slatzer understood why Marilyn was so frightened. He became even more alarmed when she revealed that Bobby had promised to marry her, but that she'd been unable to contact him by phone. 'He's been ignoring me. I've been trying to reach him on the phone,' she said, 'but I just can't get to him.'

Throughout July she had made frequent phone calls to Washington to the Justice Department switchboard but couldn't get through to Bobby. She was told she was not to contact the Kennedys again. Marilyn couldn't understand why she was being rejected.

According to what Peter Lawford told Deborah Gould, Bobby had become aware of the pressure the mob were trying to put on him and was fearful of any compromise that might arise from his involvement with Marilyn. It had even become general knowledge among the Senate that President Kennedy had told his brother to 'break it off' with Monroe. This Bobby did without a word. All that Marilyn met with was silence and rejection. It infuriated her. Slatzer warned her never to tell anyone about the diary or what was in it. But she called Peter Lawford and said, 'I've been used. I'm going public with everything.'

The legend of Marilyn Monroe has it that the intolerable depression that she was under culminated in her suicide. But was she so depressed in the last few weeks of her life?

According to Bob Slatzer, once she'd got the red diary off her chest, she settled down. He kept constantly in touch with her and on the Wednesday before she died, she'd called him with the news that she and Fox had settled their differences and work on *Something's Got to Give* was soon to restart. She'd even had to turn down an offer to have her own Las Vegas nightclub act because filming was to resume. She told Slatzer that she was very busy making plans 'for the next couple of weeks'.

She talked for a while about Bobby Kennedy, saying that the desperation she'd felt before was gone. 'I just feel he owes me an explanation for walking out on me,' she told Slatzer.

The next day, Slatzer called to tell her that he'd heard Bobby was going to be in San Francisco for the weekend. She said she'd try again to reach Bobby in Washington and then try San Francisco. Bobby arrived in San Francisco on the Friday with his family, to spend the weekend with lawyer John Bates at his ranch.

That Friday proved to be a very busy one for Marilyn. Producer Jule Styne called from New York to offer her the lead in a musical version of *A Tree Grows in Brooklyn*. She was thrilled and said she'd be in New York on Thursday when they could discuss the details. Her initial reason for going to New York was to visit her friends the Strasbergs.

A little later Sidney Skolsky called and she told him about the proposed musical and about a film she was anxious to make in which she would portray Jean Harlow. Skolsky promised to set up some screenings of a number of Harlow pictures for her, and they set a date to go to the beach together on Sunday. Then she called her designer and made an appointment for Monday as she wanted a new dress made for what she described as 'a very special party' she was planning.

During the afternoon she saw her agent, Arthur Jacobs, who was setting himself up as a producer and was going to make *What a Way to Go*, to be directed by J. Lee Thompson. Of course he wanted Marilyn to star in it and they agreed to meet with Thompson at 5 p.m. on Monday.

Mrs Murray, the housekeeper who had been specially hired by Dr Greenson to take care of Marilyn, has said, 'At least one thing is certain. On Friday Marilyn had no sombre plans for ending her life. There was too much to look forward to.'

However, she became upset in the afternoon when she tried to get through to Bobby's office again. She called Slatzer who told her Bobby was probably on his way to San Francisco. He cautioned her about Bobby again and suggested she just forget him.

'This is different,' she said. 'If he keeps avoiding me, I might just call a press conference and tell them about it.' Slatzer warned her not to threaten Kennedy, but she said, 'If he's out there, I'll get in touch with him.'

That night Marilyn was plagued by phone calls from a woman, according to Jeanne Carmen who saw Marilyn on Saturday morning. This anonymous woman said things like, 'Tramp! Leave Bobby alone or you'll be in deep trouble.'

The mystery caller has never been identified, nor the location from which she was calling, but since Marilyn's affair with Bobby was not publicly known, the caller had to be someone who moved in the necessary circles. Could she have called from Washington? After all, Marilyn had spent some of Friday trying to get through to Bobby. Could this mysterious woman simply have been making idle threats? Or was it actually a warning?

Sometime during Saturday Peter Lawford called Marilyn and invited her to his house that evening for a party. But Marilyn had other plans. She had a date that day to have dinner with Ralph Roberts. Most of the day was spent just lounging around the house. A small night table she had ordered arrived and she put it into her bedroom and arranged her bottles of pills on it. Mrs Murray was there just about all day, and for much of the time so was Pat Newcomb.

During the morning photographer Larry Schiller called in to discuss a *Playboy* cover with Marilyn. She was in the garden at the time pulling weeds. Schiller remembers how marvellous she looked and how fresh her face was, as though she 'didn't have a single worry'.

According to Mrs Murray, Marilyn had that day been 'happy, gay, alert, anything but depressed'.

From that time on, events become rather vague, if only because of the many versions of Marilyn's last hours that have been propagated. What is certain is that at about 5 p.m. Dr Greenson arrived and stayed with Marilyn in her bedroom for almost two hours. What took place in that time, or why he was there, has never been revealed. All he ever said to reporters and the police was that Marilyn was 'despondent'. If she was, what had suddenly caused it?

According to what Dr Greenson and Mrs Murray told police, at about 6 p.m. Dr Greenson suggested to Pat Newcomb that she leave. This Pat did. About half an hour later Ralph Roberts called to confirm his dinner date with Marilyn. He recalls, 'A man answered the phone. I knew it was Dr Greenson for I recognized his voice. I asked for Marilyn. He said, "She's not in right now." '

Before he left, Dr Greenson asked Mrs Murray if she would sleep over at Marilyn's that night. Usually Mrs Murray went home at nights, but she agreed to stay. All that Mrs Murray knows after that is that at 8 p.m. Marilyn said, 'Goodnight, Mrs Murray, I think I'll turn in now.' And she shut her bedroom door. Mrs Murray says that that was the last time she saw Marilyn alive.

The man to take up the story next is Peter Lawford. However, his account of his conversations with Marilyn on the phone that evening have varied over the years. Originally he said that he had called her at about seven and that she had said she wouldn't come to his house for dinner because she was sleepy and had a busy day Sunday. 'She said she felt happy and was going to bed,' said Lawford. However, over the years Earl Wilson has spoken to Lawford on several occasions and has pieced together a different account. The time now switches to 8 p.m. and Lawford is expecting Marilyn to show up at his house. She hasn't arrived so he calls her. 'What happened to you?' he asks.

Her voice is 'weird, sleepy, fuzzy'. She says that she isn't going to make it. She's too tired. Pat Newcomb wouldn't be there either. They'd had a quarrel and Pat had gone home. Then she says, 'Say goodbye to Pat, say goodbye to the President, and say goodbye to yourself, because you're a nice guy.'

Said Lawford, 'When somebody says goodbye, I figure that's terminal.'

Lawford now panics and wants to go over to see Marilyn, but his manager, Milt Ebbins says, 'You can't go over there. You're the brother-in-law of the President of the United States. Your wife's away. Let me get in touch with her doctor or lawyer. They can help her.'

'But she said goodbye to me,' protests Lawford. 'She may be dying.'

Another person who spoke to her that evening on the phone was Jeanne Carmen. She says that Marilyn called her and asked her to come over. She wasn't able to come, so Marilyn asked her for some sleeping pills. Again Miss Carmen said she couldn't get over.

Why should Marilyn ask for sleeping pills if she already had some? According to Detective Sergeant Byron's report, she must have had fifty Nembutals at her disposal, all of which had apparently been swallowed by Marilyn. But here was Marilyn asking Jeanne Carmen for sleeping pills. Were there actually any pills in her bedroom?

Ralph Roberts also received a call from her, only he was out and his answering service recorded the message. Her voice, Roberts recalls, 'sounded fuzzy and troubled'.

The official story now has it that there was nothing more anyone knew until Mrs Murray became concerned about Marilyn during the night. But at what time – midnight or 3.30 a.m.? For more than twenty years Mrs Murray has stuck to the story that it was about 3.30. The two doctors concerned always maintained that *rigor mortis* had set in by 3.40 a.m. This version, still, of course, contradicts Sergeant Clemmons's story. But now further evidence has surfaced that puts the official account in a totally unbelievable light.

Marilyn Monroe did not die at home. At some time during the night Schaefer's Ambulance Service was called to Monroe's house. According to Schaefer himself, she was alive but in a coma when they picked her up. She was rushed to Santa Monica Hospital. It's not known whether she died on the way or after they reached the hospital, and unfortunately all the records of patients coming in at that time have been destroyed. But Schaefer insists she was alive when they left her home and died sometime after that. Someone had the job of getting her dead body back home and laying her out on the bed. Who did this is not known, but it at least corroborates Sergeant Clemmons's feeling that he saw her laid out as though the whole scene had been 'arranged'.

When faced with this new evidence, Mrs Murray, now old and understandably forgetful, admitted that it was midnight when she discovered Marilyn dead, but she can't remember why she didn't call Dr Greenson until 3.30.

What complicates things even more is an incident that happened a little earlier that night. Marilyn's agent Arthur

Jacobs was, that Saturday evening, at the Hollywood Bowl with his wife Natalie. Jacobs is now dead, but according to his wife, at about 11 p.m. a message came through to Arthur saying that Marilyn was dead or on the point of dying. Yet the official story says that it was Mrs Murray who was the one who first saw Marilyn lying dead as she looked through the window, and Mrs Murray put the time at midnight.

If Mrs Jacobs is correct about the time her husband took the message, then somebody else knew about Marilyn before Mrs Murray did.

Despite a thorough search, the police never found a suicide note. Many have felt that the lack of a suicide note should have been reason enough to call for an inquest into Marilyn's death, but none was called.

However, there was, at that time in Los Angeles, a newly formed body called the Suicide Investigation Team which had been set up because of the increasing number of suicides in Los Angeles. Its function was to aid science and psychiatry in finding out why people took their own lives. Its services for the county coroner's office came free. Police Chief Parker decided to take advantage of the SIT and have them investigate Monroe's suicide. The crux was, however, it wasn't the team's job to find out the cause of death but merely to determine *why* Marilyn killed herself. Its findings were that Marilyn was despondent and 'emotionally disturbed'.

The autopsy did little more to satisfy questions over the cause of death. It was performed by Dr Thomas Noguchi. His findings were that there was a high concentration of barbiturates in her blood and liver. There was no sign of the drug in her stomach, and that made a lot of people sit up and think. The presumption was that Marilyn had swallowed almost fifty Nembutals in 'a few seconds', according to the coroner. An empty vial that had contained Nembutals was found in her room. Had she swallowed such a large number of pills, a residue should have been present in her stomach. There was none. The kidneys were also found to be clear. This should have indicated that the stomach may well have been bypassed by the drug, and the only way for that to have happened would have been by injection.

No syringe was found in the bedroom.

There are other discrepancies. It was said that almost fifty pills were taken, accounting for the enormous amount of barbiturates found in her blood and liver – enough, in fact, to kill several people. However, the label on the empty vial clearly showed that it had contained twenty-five tablets. How could she have taken almost fifty?

But what is even more inconsistent with the official report is that Marilyn was unable to swallow any amount of pills, be they five, twenty-five or fifty, without a drink. No glass or cup, empty or otherwise, was found in Marilyn's room.

Dr Noguchi knew the implications of a possible by-pass of the stomach and kidneys, and recommended to District Attorney John Miner that the organs be sent for microscopic analysis to establish conclusively if the drug had been taken orally or otherwise. The DA was eager to have the tests carried out. However, once the specimens were out of Noguchi's hands, they mysteriously disappeared, as did all the medical photos. No one was able to account for them. Despite the loss of these specimens, those who favour the suicide verdict have been quick to point out that during the autopsy Dr Noguchi found 'no needlemarks'.

There were some, however, who remained totally unconvinced that Marilyn had killed herself. One of these was Robert Slatzer who has spent thousands of dollars investigating the case with the help of private eye Milo Speriglio. Says Slatzer, 'I want to clear her name of the charge that she murdered herself.'

Through his efforts, Slatzer discovered a great deal, much of which was laughed at as being far-fetched until corroborative evidence from other quarters surfaced only recently. One of his theories which to a great many people read more like fiction than fact, was that Bobby Kennedy had in fact visited Marilyn on the afternoon of Saturday, 5 August 1962. Over that weekend, you'll remember, Bobby Kennedy and his family had gone to stay with lawyer John Bates at his ranch in San Francisco. But according to Slatzer Kennedy arrived at both Marilyn's and Peter Lawford's homes on the Saturday, although Peter Lawford never once publicly admitted Kennedy was there.

Slatzer based his assumption on what appeared to be a far-fetched piece of evidence – a so-called murder file. He claimed that he learned of it from sources within the Los Angeles Police Department. It was supposedly a 723-page report labelled *Marilyn Monroe–Murder*. It was kept somewhere down in the police vaults, but some had seen it and told Slatzer of its contents.

It included a statement made by Kennedy in which he admitted visiting Marilyn that Saturday afternoon after she managed to phone through to him. She was angry when he arrived and attacked him. He subdued her and called his doctor who just happened to be outside in the car. The doctor gave Marilyn an injection to calm her down. (If this is true, then how did Noguchi miss seeing this needlemark?) Bobby said in his deposition that it was his brother John and not he with whom Marilyn was involved. He said he'd come to Los Angeles to visit Marilyn on the President's orders because she had been annoying Jack and was beginning to embarrass him. She had threatened him with telling newspapers that she had been having affairs with both of them. Bobby claimed he had tried to assure her that she had not been snubbed, but that the Kennedys were simply being cautious as the President had to be discreet. Then he left and went to Peter Lawford's house.

Nobody believed Slatzer, even though he managed to find one woman whose mother had lived just down the road from Marilyn and had seen Bobby Kennedy and a man with a black bag go into Monroe's house. Slatzer had promised, however, to keep the woman's name a secret. His evidence was purely hearsay, but it resolved him all the more to prove that Marilyn had been murdered.

There was one other witness who could testify as to whether Bobby Kennedy had been at Marilyn's house or not – Mrs Murray. She steadfastly denied he had been there.

It seemed that Slatzer's murder file and visit by Kennedy would remain in the realms of pure supposition, until Police Chief Tom Reddin had the file found and released. It had lain hidden in the vaults for more than two decades. Its very existence had been denied by Reddin's predecessor, William Parker. At the time of Monroe's death one of the few men who could demand to see such a file was the Mayor, Sam Yorty. In fact, he did ask to see it, but was told there wasn't one. He had never believed that though, and had assumed it had been removed. As he said, 'It's easier to tell the Mayor there isn't a file rather than tell him he can't see it.'

Now the file has been made public. Unfortunately, like so many other things such as the organ specimens and the photographs of Monroe's dead body, most of it had gone missing. All that was left were a few media articles and little more. Reddin himself is convinced there was more to it. Even with valuable documents missing, it corroborates Slatzer's tale of the Marilyn Monroe murder file.

But what was there to prove that Bobby Kennedy had been to see Monroe on that Saturday?

During his marriage to Deborah Gould, Peter Lawford had revealed much. He told her that Bobby Kennedy had indeed been in Los Angeles that day and had been to both his house and Monroe's. Lawford said that Bobby had been to tell Marilyn that it was all over and she had become hysterical.

Now, at last, even Mrs Murray confesses that Bobby Kennedy did come to the house that day and that was why Marilyn had been so upset. It was immediately following Bobby's visit that Dr Greenson was called, and he spent two hours with Monroe.

Because Dr Greenson would never reveal the reason for his visit or what happened while he was there, all we can do is to look to the statement of Bobby Kennedy to the police. If Kennedy's own doctor had administered a shot to sedate Marilyn, then there must obviously have been a needlemark on Marilyn's body, whether Noguchi saw it or not. And if one injection had been given, then why not a second more lethal injection later that evening? As for any kind of a needlemark, drawings of Monroe's corpse showed a bruise around the left hip – a common location for an injection.

And if Marilyn *had* been killed by an injection, she could not have given it to herself as there was no syringe found – only the empty vial.

There still remain some contradictory points over Kennedy's visit. Police Chief Parker himself knew that Kennedy was in town and told Mayor Sam Yorty that Kennedy was at the

Beverly Hills Hotel. But John Bates, Bobby's host in San Francisco, insists that Kennedy never left his ranch the whole weekend. And Bates is a lawyer.

Someone is clearly lying.

Peter Lawford is among those who said Bobby was in Los Angeles, although publicly he always denied it. He only confided in Deborah Gould and seems to have by and large confessed truthfully to her all that happened. Yet Lawford maintained, even to Deborah Gould, that Marilyn killed herself. His version to his wife of Marilyn's phone call that Saturday evening is quite different from the versions he has given over the years. It seems that Marilyn called that night, saying she couldn't take any more and it would be better for everyone if she killed herself. He refused to take her seriously, but did add, 'For God's sake, Marilyn, don't leave any notes behind.'

According to the story he told Deborah Gould, he had gone to Marilyn's home that night following her death and had made a rough search before the police arrived. He said that he had found the suicide note and destroyed it.

Private investigator Fred Otash recalls how that night at around 3 a.m. Lawford turned up at his home asking for help. He was in shock and saying that Marilyn Monroe was dead and that Kennedy was there and was getting out of town; that Marilyn and Bobby had got into a big fight that evening and he wanted Otash to have someone go to Monroe's house and find any evidence of a relationship between Monroe and Bobby Kennedy.

If Otash has got his facts right – and he is a private eye – then according to Lawford, Bobby Kennedy had either been back to Marilyn's home that evening and 'had got into a big fight', or they had rowed on the phone.

Bobby Kennedy escaped from Los Angeles that evening by helicopter and plane back to San Francisco. But there remains an emphatic denial by lawyer John Bates that Kennedy left his ranch all weekend, despite confirmation to the contrary by Police Chief Parker, Peter Lawford, Mrs Murray, as well as Ward Wood, a neighbour of Lawford who clearly recalls seeing Kennedy at the Lawfords that Saturday afternoon.

What is certain is that there was a major effort by most of those concerned, both in Los Angeles and San Francisco, to keep Bobby Kennedy out of the picture: Lawford racing to Otash to have all evidence destroyed and then to deny emphatically Kennedy's presence that day or indeed any involvement with Marilyn; John Bates's insistence that Kennedy never left his ranch; Mrs Murray's own denial that Kennedy came that Saturday (although she now admits he was there); and Police Chief Parker's seizing of the telephone records; all these were parts of an uncoordinated plot to keep Bobby Kennedy's and his brother's names out of the case altogether. It all adds up to a massive, if bungled, cover-up that resulted in rumours that wouldn't die and questions that still beg to be fully answered. Unfortunately, many of those who could have provided the answers are now dead, including Peter Lawford, Bobby Kennedy and John Kennedy. And Bernie Spindel, the man who bugged the Lawfords' home.

Three weeks before she died, when Marilyn had called Bob Slatzer from the telephone booth in Coldwater Canyon Park, she told Slatzer that she believed her own telephone was bugged.

She was right.

In 1966 Spindel's home in New York was raided on the orders of Manhattan District Attorney Frank Hogan. Much of Spindel's equipment and tapes were seized as evidence, he was told, to prove an indictment against him on charges of illegal wire-tapping. But Spindel believed that the raid was carried out at the express command of Bobby Kennedy who was then planning to seek the nomination for the Presidency some time in the future.

Spindel sued in the New York Supreme Court for the return of the tapes, and in his affidavit he said that among the tapes was 'evidence concerning the circumstances surrounding the cause of death of Marilyn Monroe, which strongly suggest that the officially reported circumstances of her demise were erroneous'.

Spindel went to prison, believing that his tapes had been seized only to protect Bobby Kennedy because it had been discovered that Spindel had in fact tapped Monroe's phone. A member of the DA's staff even told newspaper reporters rather foolishly that 'the tapes indicated Marilyn was murdered and that somehow Bobby was involved if only as a catalyst causing someone else to do it'.

While in prison Spindel told a number of reporters and investigators that Jimmy Hoffa had hired him to bug Monroe's home, as he'd also bugged Lawford's home, all for the express purpose of gathering damaging evidence against the Kennedys.

Ironically, Lawford's and Monroe's homes were not the only ones Spindel had wired. He'd also wired his own home, according to Mrs Spindel. He had recorded the raid on his home in 1966, as well as a conversation he supposedly had face to face with Bobby Kennedy in a car. Before he died two years after the raid, Spindel claimed that Kennedy had become aware of Spindel's wiring of both Lawford's and Monroe's homes shortly before Marilyn's death and was interested in striking a deal with Spindel for the return of all tapes. He'd met Spindel in a car and offered him $25,000 to turn them over. Spindel had refused, but he had also recorded their conversation. Bobby Kennedy had no choice but to use the law to seize the tapes. But the day the DA's men raided Spindel's apartment, microphones were picking up the conversation. Mrs Spindel has revealed that one detective can be heard asking another, 'What does the Marilyn Monroe case have to do with the indictment?'

That's obviously a question that many would like to have answered. Spindel was the man who could answer that best and, apparently, did to a number of interviewers during his time in prison. Among the tapes which had been seized and which Spindel had tried to recover, was a recording of a telephone conversation that had come through from San Francisco to Los Angeles during the early hours of Sunday morning following the discovery of Marilyn's body but before the news had been announced publicly. Whether the call came to Marilyn's home or Lawford's or anybody' else's, Spindel would never reveal. That recording is now in the possession of Mrs Spindel, or so she claims, and on it can be heard the voice of the caller from San Francisco asking, 'Is she dead yet?'

As to the fate of all those tapes Spindel had recorded, a private investigator, Ralph De Toledaro, was hired by a Republican group to find them in 1968. The private eye discovered a policeman who had them and wanted $50,000 for them. De Toledaro left it to the policeman and the Republicans themselves to fix the deal. He wanted nothing more to do with it. And so the deal was made – made on the day Bobby Kennedy was assassinated. The tapes were no longer needed. The whereabouts of the tapes are no longer known.

If the question still remains – did Marilyn Monroe kill herself? – there are those who believe they have the answer. There is Sergeant Jack Clemmons who says without a doubt, 'Marilyn Monroe was murdered.'

There is author Norman Mailer who in 1975 wrote a best-selling biography of Monroe, and he has a theory for the motive. He says, 'I always felt it was ridiculous for the Kennedys to do it, to risk losing everything.' His belief is that certain members of the CIA, furious over the way the Castro assassination attempt was handled, decided to destroy the Kennedy Administration. To do this they killed Marilyn and tidied everything up to look like it was a suicide on the surface until the autopsy revealed that it was a murder. Suspicion should then fall upon the Kennedys. It was, after all, Chief Parker, who claimed he was a friend of Bobby Kennedy, who insisted on a suicide-only investigation.

Mailer's story, however, lost credibility with the press when, in 1975, he called a press conference to present his evidence in the hope of getting the DA to take an interest in re-opening the case. It was badly timed. His Monroe biography had just been published, and it looked too much like a publicity gimmick to sell his book.

Then there is Robert Slatzer who has made continual requests to the DA's office over the years to allow the Grand Jury to study the evidence. His efforts to prove that Marilyn was murdered have been so intense that he has received threats upon his life. Taking a page out of Bernie Spindel's book, he's wired his own phone and has recorded conversations with a mystery caller who has told him that there is a contract out on him. If the calls are genuine – and they could easily be fakes – what implication does that have for the question of whether or not Monroe was murdered?

In Slatzer's employ is Milo Speriglio who says without reservation, 'Marilyn Monroe was politically assassinated.' He has discovered that Marilyn kept a tape recorder in her bedroom and taped her sessions with Bobby Kennedy. Says Speriglio, 'She was murdered for these tapes and for her notebook and anything else that may have been around.'

The notebook, or red diary, was something that disappeared before the police arrived on the night Monroe died. Speriglio believes that diary is the proof he needs to show just how much of a threat Marilyn was to the Kennedys. As Slatzer has revealed, she noted down all that Bobby said concerning the Castro assassination attempt and his vendetta against Jimmy Hoffa. In 1982 Speriglio offered a reward of $80,000 dollars to anyone who could produce the missing diary and so prove that the Kennedys, or the CIA, had a reason for killing her.

There is one other possible key to what really happened on the night of Saturday 4 August and the morning following – the conversation between Dr Greenson and Marilyn Monroe that Saturday afternoon between 5 p.m. and 7 p.m.

As has been said, Dr Greenson refused to divulge what had taken place in Marilyn's bedroom during those two hours, but he did discuss it with the District Attorney, John Miner. According to Miner, Dr Greenson told him that *he could not accept that Marilyn Monroe had killed herself.* Based on what Dr Greenson told him, John Miner is of the same opinion. But for reasons of professional ethics he can't disclose what Dr Greenson said.

It is clear, then, that Dr Greenson, based on his own experiences with Marilyn, had reason to disbelieve the suicide verdict, and that his private disclosures to John Miner were enough to make even the District Attorney doubt the official verdict.

And yet no inquest was ever held; no one was ever put under oath to testify. All there was was an incomplete autopsy and an investigation in completely the wrong direction by the Suicide Investigation Team.

It is of course understandable that a psychiatrist like Dr Greenson would refuse to discuss his patients when every code in the book says not to. But surely if he couldn't believe that Marilyn killed herself, then there are other moral and ethical codes that can only be kept by breaking the professional ones.

One of the few times he ever spoke of the case was in 1975 when he was given the chance to reply to criticism aimed at him by Norman Mailer in his biography of Monroe. In a medical journal, Dr Greenson said: 'She was getting better. She was on the road to what looked to be some sort of stability. And she died - unexpectedly, suddenly.'

So the death of Marilyn Monroe remains a mystery. But what is known, despite what the legend says, is that at the time of her death Marilyn Monroe was not the basket case we've always been given to believe - her own psychiatrist affirms that. And she was not depressed and suicidal in those last days of her life. There was a lot more that went on during the whole of that Saturday and the Sunday morning than either Sergeant Clemmons or Detective Sergeant Byron could have guessed.

Once, in a desperate bid to get to the truth, one shrewd journalist called Dr Greenson on the phone and recorded his conversation. He asked Dr Greenson to talk about what had taken place at Monroe's house that Saturday when he had spent two hours alone with her.

Dr Greenson politely, but with a sense of helplessness in his voice, told the journalist, 'I can't explain myself or defend myself without revealing things I don't want to reveal. You can't draw a line and say I'll tell you this but I won't tell you that. It's a terrible position to be in to have to say, I can't talk about it, because I can't tell the whole story.

'Listen . . . talk to Bobby Kennedy.'

Ramon Navarro: The Halloween Murder

RAMON NOVARRO KNEW no politicians. He had no connections with the mafia. He wasn't on drugs. He didn't have multiple affairs. He was, by 1968, a lonely, somewhat religious bachelor of sixty-nine, without an enemy in the world. Having retired to his home in the Hollywood Hills, he was secure from the vices and lifestyles that had taken the lives of William Desmond Taylor, Thelma Todd, Lana Turner's Johnny Stompanato, Marilyn Monroe and a number of other Hollywood personalities.

But Hollywood had changed since Novarro began making films in 1917, quickly rising to become one of the truly great 'Latin' lovers of the silent screen. Indeed, Los Angeles had changed. Where once the luxurious vice of drugs was virtually exclusive to the rich and famous, by 1968 narcotics were peddled on street corners to kids. Where mobsters had once kept crime organized and practically beyond the law, street gangs and juvenile hoodlums brought terror to the streets, raising the crime rate alarmingly. Where once the immorality of the stars was kept under disinfected wraps to protect the sensitivity of the public, vice was rampant and promiscuity a virtual institution.

If the elite of Hollywood thought they were safely cocooned inside their own bed of self-bred vices, they discovered with a sickening thud that it was not so during the latter part of the Nineteen-sixties.

On 31 October 1968, Halloween's traditional trick or treat took on a new macabre meaning when Ramon Novarro was beaten to death by two kids out for Navarro's money. It was the most brutal Hollywood murder so far, heralding a new era in true movie crimes.

Novarro had not appeared in a picture for eight years, and had not been the star of a movie for twenty-eight years. His professional decline had been as traumatic for him as such failure had been for many of the great stars of the silent screen who had been unable to retain their star status once the movies began talking.

Like many such actors, Ramon Novarro had faced self-destruction in a bottle, but in his later years he had come to terms with reality, thanks in part to his deeply rooted faith founded in Mexican Catholicism. In his last years he was a lonely, gentle soul who still lived extravagantly off the immense wealth he had accumulated and maintained.

He lived in retirement slightly apart from the world, existing as something of a fine old remnant of Hollywood past that people could marvel at like a museum piece. He took no offence, and gave none. Like Garbo, he wanted to be alone, and so maintained a somewhat sad image compared to the one he had displayed in his heyday – that of a great lover both on and off the screen.

The fact was that that old image was a creation of the Hollywood star system that took hold of Ramon Samaniegos, as he was named by baptism into his church, and moulded him into Rudolph Valentino's closest rival.

He was born in Durango, Mexico, on 6 February 1899, the son of a dentist. His family fled to Los Angeles in 1914 at the time of the Mexican Civil War, but shortly after that his father died and Ramon took on the demanding role of family breadwinner. He found work as a waiter, and in some restaurants he was called upon to sing while serving tables. He also managed to get some work as a vaudeville performer, and at the age of eighteen he landed a job as a film extra in *The Hostage*, starring Wallace Reid.

More movie work followed and his dashing good looks were noticed by a number of film-makers. D.W. Griffith and Sam Goldwyn were just two who gave him screen tests. However, he continued to do just walk-ons until Marion Morgan, a vaude-ville dance director for whom he had worked as part of her troupe since 1919, suggested to Mack Sennett that Ramon perform a novelty dance in a full-length comedy, *A Small Town Idol* with Ben Turpin and Phyllis Haver. It was just a single sequence in which he wore a turban and loincloth, but it led to a featured part in Sam Goldwyn's *Mr Barnes of New York* in 1922. That in turn led to the starring role in a small independent picture, *The Rubaiyat of Omar Khayyam*, directed by Ferdinand Binney Earle. An associate of Earle, Mary O'Hara, also wrote the scenario for Metro's *The Prisoner of Zenda*, directed by Rex Ingram. At her suggestion Ingram viewed *Omar Khayyam* – one of the few who did, since it was shelved – and he was impressed with its Mexican star. He recalled that Ramon Samaniegos had in fact worked as an extra in Ingram's *The Four Horseman of the Apocalypse* which had catapulted Rudolph Valentino to stardom. Valentino was at that time unique, positively simmering with passion and sex appeal for millions of women all around the world, yet was in no way rugged as was typical of most leading men. He heralded the era of the Latin Lovers of the Silver Screen.

The first thing Ingram did after viewing *Omar Khayyam* was to cast Ramon as Rupert Hentzau in *The Prisoner of Zenda* alongside Lewis Stone and Barbara La Marr. Recognizing in Ramon some of the qualities that made women positively faint at the mention of Rudolph Valentino, Ingram signed the Mexican actor to a personal contract, changing his name to Ramon Novarro, and paying him $125 a week. He starred again with Stone and La Marr in *Trifling Women* at Metro where he went on to star in *Scaramouche* and *The Arab* in which Ramon virtually imitated Valentino's *The Sheik*.

By 1924 Ramon Novarro was a huge star and stayed on at Metro, earning $10,000 a week. Then, in 1925, he made the film for which he was always best reembered, *Ben-Hur*. He replaced George Walsh in the title role after filming had begun when Metro became Metro-Goldwyn-Mayer. Louis B. Mayer's right-hand man, Irving Thalberg, had taken over production and replaced both the leading man and the director. Consequently, Fred Niblo directed *Ben-Hur* and Ramon Novarro enjoyed the greatest triumph of his career.

The film was continually fraught with problems and took for ever to make. By the time it was all over, Ramon experienced even greater personal traumas. In 1926 he lost two dear friends – Barbara La Marr and Rudolph Valentino.

He had starred numerous times with La Marr, who was billed

as 'The Girl Who Is Too Beautiful'. Shortly before he began *Ben-Hur* they made their last film together, *Thy Name Is Woman*. Both Novarro and La Marr projected on-screen images of passionate people. For Ramon it was pure fantasy. He never was a great lover in real life, but La Marr lived up to her image and more. She boasted that she never wasted more than two hours on sleep at night having 'better things to do'. She had dozens of lovers as well as six husbands in total. She died aged twenty-nine from a drug overdose. She was one of Hollywood's genuine addicts, hopelessly incapable of getting through the day without a fix. Her regular supplier of cocaine was 'The Count', who had also put Mabel Normand on the road to self-destruction.

With his own lifestyle far removed from that of La Marr's, Navarro was far more shaken over the death of Rudolph Valentino. Despite what might have seemed to have been competition between the two, Rudy and Ramon were close friends. Neither man ever lived up to his screen image, and Ramon never took his seriously. Such was their amusement over their supposed passionate private lives that Rudy gave Ramon a gift that positively mocked their images – a black lead phallic-shaped ornament engraved with Valentino's signature in silver. When Rudy died apparently from peritonitis, Ramon treasured the rude object in memory of his friend. Ironically, the lead phallus would play a grotesque and bizarre part in the death of Ramon Novarro more than forty years later.

The first time the movie audience heard Ramon Novarro's voice was when he sang 'Pagan Love Song' to Renée Adorée in *The Pagan* in 1930. One thing was sure; Ramon Novarro had a beautiful operatic voice, and he sang again in *Devil May Care*, a Napoleonic costume drama with Technicolor sequences. He continued singing in his pictures, but as a talking actor he was a disaster.

'Frankly', said *Picturegoer*, 'Ramon is one of the disappointments of the Talkies.'

He began to consider his future in movies. Like many stars who discovered that suddenly they were not the darlings of the audiences any more, he hit the bottle with a vengeance. It was perhaps the one vice he ever indulged in and alcohol became a continual problem for him. He took refuge in a monastery, losing himself in his faith for a while as he contemplated his future. He seriously considered retiring from movies and taking up opera-singing. But MGM persuaded him to stay with them when they offered him a new seven-year contract in 1932.

But his career continued to decline and in 1934 MGM tore up his contract. He fled to London to star in a musical at the Palladium, *A Royal Exchange*, and spoke bitterly about Hollywood. He returned to the movie capital to write, produce and direct a Spanish-speaking picture, *Contra la Corriente*, but did not star in it. Then in 1937 he made *The Sheik Steps Out* for Republic, kidding his old movie image. The studio was delighted with it and signed him to do four more pictures, but after just one more, *A Desperate Adventure*, he asked Republic to release him. They did, and the realization that his days as a leading man were all but over caused him to drown his sorrows with booze again. On numerous occasions he was picked up by the police for drunken driving.

He considered retiring to a monastery for the rest of his life, but his fondness for alcohol came between him and his religious beliefs.

In 1940 he went to Europe and starred in and directed a French movie, *La Comédie de Bonheur*, and then he returned to Mexico for a Spanish-speaking picture *La Virgen que forjó una Patria*. He didn't work again until 1949 when he did some character acting in four films over a period of little more than a year and disappeared again. He re-emerged briefly in 1960 to do a cameo in George Cukor's *Heller In Pink Tights*. It was his last picture. Resigning himself to permanent retirement at the age of sixty-one, he locked himself away in his Hollywood Hills home, forever contemplating the prospect of a monastic life. Death, however, was soon to rob him of his dream.

Paul and Tom Ferguson were two brothers from Chicago. Both still in their teens, they lived on their wits and talent for petty theft. They were just small-time hustlers; two punks hungry for easy money who didn't give a damn for anyone or anything.

They'd heard that the old movie star, Ramon Novarro, had thousands of dollars stashed away somewhere in his Hollywood home. Novarro was sixty-nine. He lived alone. It seemed like easy pickings.

Perhaps it was their freakish sense of humour that caused them to pick Halloween to call on Novarro. Only they didn't knock at the door dressed in Halloween costume. They simply broke in and found Novarro alone as predicted.

From that moment on they engaged in a bloody orgy of violence that was unprecedented in Hollywood history. They could have just subdued the old man and taken his money, but they didn't. They mercilessly and relentlessly beat him to a pulp until his blood splattered the many souvenirs that decorated his home as reminders of his glorious days in pictures.

They stripped him naked and continued to beat him. Then they found Rudolph Valentino's gift to Ramon – the black lead phallus. They forced it down his throat until he finally choked on his own blood and died. Then they ransacked the place and found $5,000 in cash.

This time there were no political overtones, no reprisals from the Mob, no insanely jealous lovers suspected of foul play. The two cretins responsible for the barbaric death of one of Hollywood's gentlest souls simply got what they came for, and left enough clues for the police to apprehend and arrest them. They were both convicted of murder and sent away for life.

Novarro had few friends when he died, but those who knew him were thunderstruck, and the whole Hollywood community suddenly became aware of their vulnerability. But if they needed convincing that this was not just an isolated case and that even the demi-gods and goddesses of tinsel town needed to protect themselves from thugs weaned on the new drug culture, then all the evidence they needed was forthcoming in just a year with a Hollywood murder that made even the death of Ramon Novarro – the original *Ben-Hur* – seem mild in comparison.

CASE 10

The Sharon Tate Massacre

SATURDAY MORNING, 9 August 1969 – Winifred Chapman arrived at the home of film director Roman Polanski on Cielo Drive at eight-thirty. She'd come, as usual, to clean house. But even before she'd reached the front door she was met by a sight that sent shock waves through her. Lying slumped on the lawn was the dead body of a man, his corpse punctured and blood-drenched.

In stupefied horror she staggered to the front door, to find the word 'PIG' splashed irregularly over it in blood. Her heart froze, but even then she was still not prepared for the carnage that awaited her indoors.

In the lounge, Polanski's pregnant wife, actress Sharon Tate, lay dead, mutilated beyond belief, her briefs and bra soaked in blood that had pumped from the horrifying wounds in her neck, breast and ripped-open stomach. A rope was tight around her neck, leading to another body, that of Sharon's one-time lover, Jay Sebring. The noose was tight around his neck too. He also had received several stab wounds and had been shot in the back. Outside, through the patio windows in Sharon's bedroom, could be seen yet another corpse, a woman also stabbed repeatedly, her blood turning the lawn scarlet.

Winifred Chapman roamed the house in a daze, taking in the scene, unable to find the right emotions with which to respond. Finally, she called the police. They arrived at nine-thirty. Clearly, they reasoned, this bore all the hallmarks of a ritual killing, and the whole of Los Angeles went into a state of panic.

At midday Polanski's agent, Bill Tennant, arrived to identify the bodies and was physically sick. Then he put through a call to Polanski, still in London.

'Roman, there's been a disaster at the house,' explained Tennant in a shaky voice. 'Sharon is dead. And Wojtek. And Gibby and Jay. There's been a slaughter.'

Polanski trembled with shock and fear. 'I'm coming,' he said.

He booked a flight home and arrived at Los Angeles airport on Sunday night and was immediately engulfed by the press. His friend producer Gene Gutowski was with him and had astutely arranged for a car from Paramount to meet them and take them straight to the studio.

The newspapers were suddenly full of all manner of bizarre stories concerning the murder. As horrific as it already was, they printed stories of Sharon Tate having her breasts cut off and her child ripped from her belly. The killing of Tate hadn't quite come to that, but nevertheless the whole episode seemed grotesquely ritualistic.

Theories were quickly formulated. The dead man on the front lawn was Wojtek Frykowski, a dealer in narcotics. Police began questioning the movie-star friends of Polanski and Frykowski.

There followed a series of murders in Los Angeles. On the Sunday night there was a double killing that looked like the same handiwork as Tate's murderers. The day after William Lennon, father of the singing Lennon Sisters, was shot dead.

One theory had it that Polanski had hired someone or some people to kill his wife and Sebring after discovering that they were having an affair. Polanski had the perfect alibi in that he was in London at the time, but that only served to make the police suspect him all the more. But Polanski refused to talk to the police until after Sharon's funeral on Wednesday, when over a hundred people attended the service at the Holy Cross Cemetery in Culver City. Among those paying their last respects were Steve McQueen, Lee Marvin, Kirk Douglas, Warren Beatty, Peter Sellers, Yul Brynner and James Coburn. Polanski, dark glasses hiding his elfin face, broke down and cried several times.

He finally allowed police to question him the following Saturday, by which time they were harking back to their primary theory that the massacre had something to do with narcotics. A large quantity of drugs had been found at the house and both Sebring and Sharon had a history of drug abuse. Polanski was dropped as a suspect.

Then, in December, police arrested a group of drug-crazed lunatics who blindly answered to every beck and call of their self-styled Messianic leader – Charles Manson.

There have been few men more evil than Charlie Manson. He may not have murdered as many people as did Nero or Hitler, but then he wasn't born into immediate power as was Nero, nor was he the genius some say Hitler was. Manson was a bungler in crime who rose to the status of cult leader only with the help of drugs. He had been in and out of prison for most of his life. In 1960 he was incarcerated in a Californian prison and there he began to sow the bitter seeds that would lead to his eventual so-called Messiahship. Even behind bars he discovered the heavy sound of drug-rock music that had become part of the Californian culture in the mid-sixties. He took to keeping company with drug offenders, a totally different class of convict from the hardened murderers and rapists he had known all his life. This new breed of con was generally well educated and more interested in peace and love than violence.

In March 1967, aged thirty-two, Manson was paroled and put out on the streets of San Francisco. It was the Mecca of flower-power and the hippie culture where beautiful people grew their hair long and dropped acid and smoked dope. Manson grew his hair and joined the new wave of drop-outs, hustling for LSD and giving it free to the youngsters he met on the street. Before long he had a following, mostly of teenage runaway girls and small-time thieves. Through their doped-up eyes he was a Messiah who took care of them and they of him. 'Charlie is in love with us and we are all in love with Charlie,' one of his female disciples once said. 'He writes songs for us and sings them with the voice of an angel.'

As his movement grew, he took them off to Los Angeles where they took over the Spahn Ranch in the hills. He led his freaked-out disciples in sexual activities, witchcraft, drug-taking, Jesus-freaking and rituals involving the shedding of blood. There wasn't anything his disciples wouldn't do for him.

He had aspirations of being a rock star and succeeded in integrating himself with some of the elite of Los Angeles rock music, including Frank Zappa, Dennis Wilson (of The Beach Boys) and record producer Terry Melcher, the son of Doris Day. Melcher in fact arranged for Manson to have an audition with a recording company, but the drug-cult leader could barely play the guitar and certainly couldn't sing a note. The audition being

The death of Marilyn Monroe in 1962 is a continuing mystery.

Ramon Novarro, seen here in the title role of *Ben-Hur* (1926), was brutally murdered in 1968 — long after his screen career was ended.

The death of Sharon Tate in 1969 at the hands of the Manson
'family' was probably the most bestial murder in Hollywood history.

Sal Mineo, who was stabbed to death in 1976 as he returned home after rehearsal.

The career of Gig Young, seen (*left*) in *Ask Any Girl*, ended in tragedy with a double killing. Ironically, his final film (*below*) was called *Game of Death*.

a failure, Melcher avoided Manson at all costs.

Manson, determined to pursue his musical career, turned up at Melcher's house at 10050 Cielo Drive. Melcher rented the sumptuous house, which was situated on a remote hillside above Benedict Canyon, from movie agent Rudi Altobelli. Manson begged Melcher to give him another chance at an audition but Melcher told him that he had a great deal to learn before he could even think of another audition. Manson left the house, bent on revenge, and returned to the Spahn Ranch to further incite his mind-blown disciples into a sadistic sexual fervour.

Early in 1969 Terry Melcher moved out of Altobelli's house and in moved Roman Polanski and his wife, actress Sharon Tate. Their rent was a staggering $3,000 a month, but Polanski could afford it. An immigrant from Poland, he had directed a number of highly successful motion pictures including *Repulsion, Dance of the Vampires* and *Rosemary's Baby*. He was Hollywood's new golden boy behind the camera.

As for Sharon, she was an attractive blonde, short on talent but strong on sex appeal. She was the oldest of three daughters of Colonel Paul Tate. She was born in Dallas in 1943 and raised in numerous parts of the States wherever her father's military work took them. As a teenager she won a succession of beauty contests. She was still in high school when her father was stationed near Los Angeles. With dreams of being a movie star, she often hitchhiked into the city and hung around studios, hoping some talent scout or producer would spot her.

Somehow she managed to find an agent willing to give her a chance, and he succeeded in getting her on to a few television commercials. She was spotted by producer Martin Ransohoff who reputedly told her, 'Honey, you've got it. If you let me, I'll make you a star.' She signed a contract with him and landed several small roles in his films and TV shows.

Contrary to the image she projected she was not particularly promiscuous. She did fall in love with an out-of-work French actor and lived with him for two years until he beat her up so badly that she had to undergo emergency treatment in hospital. Then she met and fell in love with Jay Sebring, hair stylist to the stars. She was impressed with the way his clients seemed to depend on him so much. That was probably because he was supplying many of them with drugs, particularly LSD. Consequently, he introduced Sharon to the shady world of narcotics. This was to Sebring's liking because he was keen to practise his perverse sexual vices on her. Under the influence of drugs she willingly submitted to his sado-masochistic tendencies. She was no longer such an innocent, semi-virtuous girl. Her real weakness was that she was willing to do anything for the man she loved.

She was still living with Sebring when she went to London with Martin Ransohoff in the summer of 1966. At a party she met Roman Polanski. Ransohoff was particularly keen to talk to Polanski about doing a horror film, having been impressed with *Repulsion*. In fact, Ransohoff had produced a picture called *Eye of the Devil*, a story of witchcraft starring David Niven and Deborah Kerr. Sharon had also featured in the picture. Ransohoff wanted to follow up with another more stylish horror picture.

Polanski was interested as he had been working on a script which was actually a spoof of horror films and Ransohoff immediately promised to produce it provided that Sharon appeared in the film. Sharon didn't even like Polanski at first. They met on numerous occasions at social events and his rather abrasive attitude turned her off completely.

When production began on the spoof horror picture, *Dance of the Vampires*, her response to Polanski changed. She had no illusions about her acting ability, and he exercised great authority on the set and gave her a strong hand in guiding her through her performance. She responded to his direction, and warmed to him personally. It helped also that Polanski appeared in the film, playing Sharon's vampire lover. Before long, they were lovers away from the set.

They began living together, commuting much of the time between America and England, and on 20 January 1968 they were married in London. Then they returned to Los Angeles where Sharon was starring in *The Valley of the Dolls*. Her career was taking shape, and Polanski was basking in the success of *Rosemary's Baby*. But their marriage was failing: Polanski couldn't help pursuing other women. Sharon, determined to save the marriage, felt that a baby might solve their problems.

She pestered Roman to try for a baby, and he eventually gave in. During December 1968, she conceived.

She gave up using drugs altogether and went to Rome to make a picture. By now she and Polanski had moved into Altobelli's house on Cielo Drive. It was a veritable Hollywood mansion, protected by electronic gates at the top of the drive and surrounded by sprawling gardens and a swimming pool. To one side of the property was a sheer drop into a canyon.

Many famous names were among the Polanskis' friends, including Steve McQueen, Jane and Peter Fonda and Warren Beatty. Jay Sebring, Sharon's former lover, was also a close friend and kept the Polanski family supplied with drugs. Another, Wojtek Frykowski, frequented the place – he was an old friend of Roman from his days in Poland. Frykowski had a regular girlfriend, American coffee heiress Abigail Folger, and he, too, pushed drugs.

Shortly after Sharon and Roman moved in, there came another visitor. It was Charles Manson. He had come expecting to find Terry Melcher. Polanski was away at the time but Jay Sebring was there with Sharon. They turned Manson away; he left, vowing vengeance upon them as he had done upon Melcher. Only this time, he would fulfil his promise.

Sharon awoke at nine in the morning, and put a call through to London, trying to reach Polanski. She was going crazy and wanted his friends, Wojtek Frykowski and Abigail Folger, out of the house. They were there at Roman's request to look after Sharon while he was in London on business. But her two minders were constantly stoned and continuously arguing. She couldn't take any more, and besides, she was angry that Roman was taking so long away from home. It was Friday, 8 August and the baby was due in about another month. She couldn't stand the strain.

But she couldn't get through to Polanski that morning, and so she left a message. When he did call back, they argued. Polanski refused to order his friends out of the house and promised he'd be home soon.

That evening Jay Sebring came by. His visit was a welcome

relief from the tense atmosphere her unwanted guests were causing. Frykowski and Abigail had argued again and Abigail, dressed in her nightgown, took to her bedroom and dosed herself up with valium. Frykowski was alone in the spacious living room, lying in a drugged heap on the sofa, his multi-coloured jeans and purple shirt crumpled and sweat-stained. Sharon, in bra and panties, her belly swollen, sat in the middle of her bed while Sebring, in a blue shirt and slacks, sat on the edge puffing marijuana.

Not one of them seems to have noticed the sound of a car coming up the driveway and stopping near the house. From the car emerged four people – disciples of Charlie Manson. One was a man, Charles Watson, a one-time star football player who had dropped out of college in 1967 and, high on drugs, joined the Manson family. He was totally obedient to his master. His orders that night were to get rid of anyone found at 10050 Cielo Drive. Dirty, tattered, with a scruffy beard and long hair, he came packing a pistol in his belt, a coil of rope around his neck and a bayonet in his fist. The other three intruders were girls – Susan Atkins, Patricia Krenwinkle and Linda Kasabian. They carried knives. Their faces were ravaged by drugs and venereal disease and belied their youth.

Watson circled the house, peering through windows, and then returned and gave orders to the girls. They crept up to the porch while Watson went to a window and climbed inside. He made his way to the living room and saw Frykowski sleeping on the sofa. Hearing voices, he crept to the front door and let Atkins and Krenwinkle in. Kasabian remained outside to keep watch.

Watson led the two girls to the living room. Drawing his gun, he poked Frykowski in the back and ordered, 'Get up.' Frykowski awoke to find himself staring down the barrel of a gun. 'Don't move a muscle,' ordered Watson.

'Who do you . . .'

'Shut up!'

'But . . .'

'Shut up or you're a dead man.'

'Who are you?' Frykowski finally managed to ask.

'I'm the Devil,' replied Watson, 'and I'm here to do the Devil's business.'

Watson sent the two girls to search the other rooms. Atkins found herself in Abigail's room. Abigail opened her eyes dreamily, saw the vague figure of Atkins, and smiled. Atkins returned to the living room, as did Krenwinkle who reported there was no one in the kitchen or serving quarters. Then the girls tied Frykowski up and returned to Abigail's room. Again she smiled, but this time her expression soon changed to one of stark terror as Atkins leaped on to the bed and put a knife to Abigail's throat.

'Get up and go into the living room,' ordered Atkins. 'Just do as I say and you won't get hurt.'

While Krenwinkle forced Abigail into the living room with a knife at her back, Atkins found Sharon and Sebring. She burst in, crying, 'Hurry, they need you in the living room. Something terrible has happened.'

Completely fooled and surprised, Sharon and Sebring hurried to the living room and found Watkins pointing his gun at the trussed Frykowski, and Krenwinkle holding a knife to Abigail.

'What is this?' cried Sharon.

She turned on her heel to escape to the bedroom, but Atkins blocked her route, threatening to slice her belly open with the knife.

'Over to the fireplace,' shouted Watson. 'On your stomachs.'

'You people are crazy,' cried Sebring.

'For God's sake, do what he says,' pleaded Frykowski. 'He told me he'll shoot me if you don't do as he says.'

Sharon, Abigail and Sebring moved over to the fireplace. 'Lie down,' demanded Atkins. 'On your stomachs. Hands behind your backs.'

'I can't,' cried Sharon. 'Can't you see I'm pregnant?'

Her pleas were in vain. Watson and the three girls were seemingly possessed and crazy for blood. 'Lie on your belly like she said,' shouted Watson.

'Be reasonable, for Christ's sake,' begged Sebring. 'The woman'll hurt herself.'

'Don't talk to me about Christ,' said Watson, and then he shot Sebring in the back. Sharon and Abigail began screaming hysterically.

'Now do what I tell you,' said Watson. 'And cut that noise. Who's got money?'

'She does,' said Frykowski, indicating Abigail.

'Where?' demanded Atkins.

'In the bedroom, in my purse,' said Abigail.

'Get it,' Watson told Atkins.

Atkins disappeared and shortly returned with the purse which she gave to Abigail who then turned out all the money she had – $72. She also handed over her credit cards and begged them to take anything else they wanted but to leave them alone. Sebring lay on the floor, still alive, twitching. Then he gave one final frothing cough and died. Sharon was now on the floor. Abigail fell to her hands and knees.

Watson ordered Atkins to find a towel and tie Frykowski up so he could use the rope for another purpose. While Atkins did as she was told, Watson tied a loop around Sebring's neck, made two more loops which he put around Sharon and Abigail's necks, and threw the other end over a ceiling beam. He pulled hard and as the nooses tightened around Sharon and Abigail they were forced to their feet.

'You're all going to die,' taunted the crazed Watson. 'Pigs! Look at you,' he said to Sharon, 'you look like a pig with that belly of yours. A piggie. A sow.' He was shouting hysterically, overcome with frenzy. He took the knife from Krenwinkle and sank it into Sebring's body several times. Watson was now covered in blood from the corpse of Sebring, and he turned on Sharon, holding the bloody knife to her. 'You will die like a pig.'

Abigail screamed. Watson threw the knife back to Krenwinkle, then saw that Frykowski was working his hands free of the towel. 'Kill him,' he shouted at Atkins.

Atkins went at him with the knife, but he rolled out of the way. 'No, not me,' he cried. Watson kicked him back down on to the sofa and Atkins lunged at him again. He caught her arm and wrestled with her, tearing out her hair. Suddenly he felt the knife in his side and then again in his leg. He let go of Atkins and dragged himself towards the door. Watson leapt on to him, hitting him over the head with his pistol. The handle broke and Frykowski managed to stand. He staggered towards the door, his face covered in blood.

Watson aimed his gun and fired twice. Frykowski caught both bullets in the back, but he managed to make it to the front door, collapsing on the porch. He expected Watson to come after him, but Watson, assuming Frykowski was dead, remained where he was. The Pole dragged himself through a hedge and on to the lawn.

Meanwhile, with Watson's attention diverted, Abigail escaped from her noose and headed for the hall. Watson saw her and screamed to his girls, 'Get her!'

Krenwinkle was immediately on to Abigail, plunging her knife into her back. She fell and Krenwinkle lunged at her again but missed. Suddenly Watson was over Abigail, and he sank his bayonet into her belly. Sharon screamed and Abigail managed to get up and run, making it through the French doors of Sharon's bedroom and out towards the swimming pool. But Watson caught her, grabbing her by the hair and running her through with his bayonet. He stabbed her over and over in a frenzy, and Krenwinkle joined in. There was still a flicker of life in Abigail, but Krenwinkle kept on stabbing her even after that last flicker had gone out.

Arriving back in the living room, Watson saw that Sharon was forcing off her noose while Atkins stood by simply shouting. 'Kill her!' he screamed.

Atkins reached for Sharon's neck and they toppled over with Sharon pinning Atkins to the floor.

'I said kill her,' screeched Watson.

'I can't,' replied Atkins, unable to keep Sharon still.

'My baby, I want my baby,' cried Sharon.

'Help me,' called Atkins.

Watson rushed over and plunged his bayonet into Sharon's stomach. She moaned and lay still. Atkins sank her knife into Sharon's left breast and then in went the bayonet again. Finally Sharon slid off Atkins, who continued to plunge her knife into Sharon repeatedly. Intent on cutting out the baby and giving it to Manson as a prize, Atkins tried to slice Sharon's belly open, but the knife stuck. She tried again but Watson was calling for them all to leave.

Atkins met Watson and Krenwinkle outside, but there was no sign of their lookout, Linda Kasabian. She had fled much earlier. They headed for the car and as they passed by Frykowski, now dead, Watson plunged his bayonet three or four times into the body. Then he remembered something he was supposed to do. 'Charlie said to leave a message,' he said.

'I'll do it,' said Atkins, and ran back into the house. She picked up the towel in the living room and soaked it in the blood that was still pumping out of Sharon. Atkins stabbed her one more time, and the pumping stopped. Sharon Tate was dead.

Gripping the blood-drenched towel, Atkins ran to the white front door and smeared on it the word 'PIG', then hurled the towel back into the living room. It landed on Sebring's face. Another idea struck her. She tied the noose back round Sharon's neck and dragged the body so that the rope became taught between Sebring, who still had one end of it around him, and Sharon. Then she rejoined her companions and they drove away.

They had shown no mercy, felt no remorse, no conscience. Theirs had been a mission of slaughter, as ordered by Charlie Manson whom they worshipped and obeyed without question. When Manson and his following were finally rounded up in December 1969, and ultimately sentenced to life imprisonment, Manson's disciples remained just as loyal, and remain so today even in prison. It's almost incomprehensible, but the three girls who had accompanied Watson on that late Friday night had all once been normal, decent kids, but became turned on to Manson's own gospel through drugs.

Manson and his following never expressed any kind of guilt over the Sharon Tate massacre. For them, it was virtually something to boast about. Before the grand jury, Susan Atkins gave a detailed testimony of what happened that night with alarming clarity.

Police had managed to link Manson and his 'family' to the Sharon Tate incident through a series of other murder investigations. Two nights after Tate, Sebring and the others were slaughtered, Manson sent his disciples to a couple who were virtual neighbours to Polanski, and had them killed also. Other crimes committed by the 'family' around that time included the murder of a musician on Manson's orders, and the decapitation of a Hollywood stuntman performed personally by Manson.

There were other atrocities, and Manson was sentenced to the gas chamber. However, because of a change in the law concerning capital punishment, Manson was finally given a total of nine life sentences. His disciples, also imprisoned, continued to worship and devote themselves to him.

Charlie Manson was responsible for the most grizzly, pointless and totally bestial murders in Hollywood history. Almost as soon as the news broke about the massacre on Cielo Drive, the defences went up all over town. Jerry Lewis hired bodyguards to watch over him night and day. Frank Sinatra took on a hired gunman, and other movie and music stars began toting guns and letting ferocious guard dogs loose in their grounds. Since that time many Hollywood homes have become fortresses and intruders, no matter how innocent, are likely to be shot at. Such is the price the rich and famous in both the film and the music world have had to pay to ensure their well-being as the crime rate in America has dramatically risen.

Bruce Lee: A Macabre
Romantic Notion?

THEY CALLED HIM the king of kung-fu. He was described as the
'fittest man in the world'. His body was his 'pride and obsession'.
He lived on a special diet and trained as though every fight was
his last. Then, suddenly, unbelievably, Bruce Lee died in Hong
Kong on 20 July 1973. At thirty-two, the fittest man in the world
was dead, and no one seemed to know why.

He had only just achieved international superstar status
through the Hollywood star-making machine. It had long been
his ambition, and for a time he had thought that he would never
make it. He'd been born in San Francisco to Eurasian parents
who were members of a Chinese opera company touring the
States. He was raised in Hong Kong and became a child actor in
Mandarin films. He also grew to be a young thug, taking to the
streets in search of a fight, ready to use chains and knives.
Inevitably, his fighting prowess led him to take a course in
kung-fu. He became fanatical about it and went on to study
almost every form of fighting technique until he was a true
master of the martial arts.

But his greatest dream was of being a Hollywood movie star.
He once said, 'To most people, including the Mandarin actors
and actresses, Hollywood is like a magic kingdom. It's beyond
everyone's reach.'

It came within reach when, in later years, he spent time in the
United States teaching self-defence. In 1964 he was seen doing a
demonstration at Long Beach by hairdresser Jay Sebring (one of
the victims in the Sharon Tate massacre). Among Sebring's
customers was television producer William Dozier who later
created the 'Batman' TV series. At that time Dozier was looking
for an Oriental martial artist for a TV series, 'The Green
Hornet'. Sebring told him about Bruce Lee, and consequently
Lee landed his first Hollywood role in the spoof adventure series
which, amazingly, was never aired in Britain (to the chagrin of

all Bruce Lee's British fans). His regular slot in 'The Green Hornet' led to guest appearances in such shows as 'Ironside', and to small parts in movies, most notably in *Marlowe* in which, in one dazzling scene, he demolishes James Garner's office using just his hands and feet.

He began teaching kung-fu to some of Hollywood's elite, including Steve McQueen, James Coburn and James Garner. Then he landed a featured role in the feature-length pilot of the successful 'Longstreet' series, and things started looking really promising when he was approached to play the lead in a new western-martial arts TV series from Warner Bros. called 'Kung-Fu'. He hung all his hopes and aspirations on it, but he was dropped in favour of David Carradine.

He felt rejected and despondent, and gladly accepted a call from Chinese producer Raymond Chow to star in a cheap martial arts picture, *The Big Boss*, in Hong Kong. It turned out to be a sensational hit, and *Fist of Fury* followed. He was suddenly Hong Kong's biggest star, and he went on to star in and direct *The Way of the Dragon*. It scored not just in the East, but in the West too, and a whole spate of kung-fu movies appeared and swamped the cinemas of the world. Suddenly Hollywood was taking a closer look at the Chinese boy whom they'd let get away, and Warner Bros. signed him for *Enter the Dragon*. It was a phenomenal success and Bruce Lee became the hottest property around.

MGM were trying to persuade him to star with Elvis Presley in a picture, Carlo Ponti wanted him to co-star with Sophia Loren, and Warner Bros. had a dozen scripts they wanted him to look at. But what he really wanted to do was to make *Game of Death* which he'd long planned. Warners offered to produce it for him provided he made five more films for them and promising him $100,000 a year until such time as he completed all five films.

But it all came too late for him. After filming only a couple of fight scenes for *Game of Death* he died in Hong Kong. It seemed inconceivable that the fittest man in the world could have just suddenly died. Speculation began immediately, and it didn't help when it was discovered that there had been a cover-up.

The initial report was that Lee had gone to bed on the evening of 20 July complaining of a headache. He was later discovered barely breathing and with hardly any pulse. He was rushed to Hong Kong's Queen Elizabeth Hospital where doctors fought to pull him out of a coma. His wife Linda was waiting in the corridor with Raymond Chow when the news came, and it was left to Chow to announce to the waiting reporters at 11.30 p.m., 'He's gone.'

Four days later *The Star* newspaper in Hong Kong declared that Lee had not been taken from his own home, nor discovered by his wife. He had been found unconscious by actress Betty Ting Pei, in *her* bed at *her* apartment. She emphatically denied the story and Raymond Chow when pressed to make a statement refused any comment. That only served to heighten everyone's suspicions.

The autopsy was not much help. It revealed that Lee's brain had swollen alarmingly for no apparent reason. The report ruled out a brain haemorrhage because none of the vessels in the brain were blocked or broken. Small traces of cannabis were found in the stomach, causing a tidal wave of stories about drug abuse. Theories arose from all quarters over Lee's death – he'd had too much sex; he'd been hacked to death by a gang of thugs; he wasn't really dead at all and was due to reappear a year later in America!

The police weren't interested in any of these wild stories. That is, until a suspicious-looking parcel was found, written on which were the words, 'Betty Ting knows the cause of Bruce Lee's death'. The parcel had all the outward appearance of a bomb, but it turned out to be empty. When three similar packages were found later, though, each with a written message – one of which read, 'Revenge for Bruce Lee' – the Hong Kong Government ordered a full-scale inquiry.

Lee had been buried in Seattle on 31 July, following a symbolic funeral in Hong Kong six days earlier. The inquest began on 3 September. As with Thomas Ince almost fifty years earlier, there was no further opportunity to examine the body. But what did surface at the inquest was the truth about Lee's whereabouts when he died.

Betty Ting Pei admitted that he had died at her apartment. She had given him a tablet of Equagesic before he went to bed with a headache. Nothing more was made of the matter of the cover-up. It was eventually agreed that Lee had died from 'acute cerebral oedema [brain swelling], due to the hypersensitivity to either meprobanate or aspirin or a combination of the two found in Equagesic'. It was, they said, 'a very rare case'. The coroner delivered a verdict of 'death by misadventure'.

But that did not satisfy everyone. Although most of the wild theories that had materialized immediately following Lee's death vanished equally as quickly, there were certain rumours that wouldn't go away, and still persist today. These enduring rumours claimed that Lee had been murdered.

The world of movies is one of make-believe – it is by definition a land of fantasy. It's never been unusual for fantasy to become confused with reality. That's why there has been so much scepticism over the murder theories about the deaths of Thomas Ince and Marilyn Monroe. Those cases, however, speak for themselves. But it's undeniable that all too often the question of murder hangs over the deaths of certain movie stars because of little more than a macabre romantic notion. It's as though idols of the screen must not be allowed to die a natural death. That's why there were murder rumours immediately following the death of the Silent Screen's most popular Latin Lover, Rudolph Valentino.

Valentino was in essence a complete fantasy. The smouldering love-making of Valentino's screen reflection was a total lie. It was purely the magic that he and the camera were able to create. In reality he was a disastrous lover. He married twice, both times to lesbians, and he apparently never played around on the side. Yet even certain stars of Hollywood found it impossible to differentiate between Valentino's screen image and the man himself. Following his funeral, at which thousands of sobbing women thronged the streets, actress Pola Negri claimed that she was to have been the next Mrs Valentino, while starlet Marion Kay Brenda announced tht Rudy had proposed to her the evening before he fell ill.

The cause of Valentino's death was an inflamed appendix. He had been rushed to hospital and given an emergency operation, but had died on 23 August at ten minutes past noon. The word quickly spread that Valentino had in fact been murdered – poisoned with arsenic by a 'well-known New York society girl' whom he'd enjoyed a brief affair with while in New York promoting his last film, *The Son of the Sheik*. According to the rumour, he had ditched her and returned to Hollywood, little knowing that the jilted woman would take revenge for her heartbreak.

It turned out that the story had been fabricated by a newspaper to sell more copies. But murder rumours persisted, one of which claimed that Rudy had been shot dead by a cheated husband. There was no doubt, however, that Valentino had died from an ordinary, normal, totally unromantic illness.

It would seem that the kind of bizarre romanticism that arouses the emotions of adoring fans who refuse to believe that such a god could possibly die from natural causes is exactly what followed in the wake of Bruce Lee's death. Only the trouble is, those rumours won't go away, not because they simply float on the air of the kind of hero worship that Lee's screen persona still enjoys thirteen years after this death, but because there are people who firmly believe he was murdered.

Two theories endure. One concerns the so-called 'delayed death strike', or 'vibrating palm' as it is also known. This is supposed to be a secret method of killing practised by only a few exponents. Apparently, they can convert their internal energies into a wave of vibrations. They then simply touch the intended victim who will die at a predetermined time – the victim could die any time up to ten years later. Those who favour this theory believe that Lee may have been killed by a Shaolin monk or a Ninja for exploiting the once-hidden secrets of kung-fu.

The other murder theory was put forward by Los Angeles karate instructor Ben Block who believes that 'foul play' was definitely the cause of Lee's death. He reasons that Lee may well have been poisoned with a secret herbal drug known only to Chinese herbalists and which would not have been detected at the autopsy. He maintains that these herbalists have many medicinal herbs which the West has never heard of. He does not, however, care to guess at who the killer was.

To date, no evidence has been forthcoming to prove either of these murder theories. It's all speculation, unless there is someone who knows something and isn't saying. For the time being, it continues to look like nothing more than a macabre romantic notion. But while the question remains, you can't help asking it!

CASE 12
Sal Mineo:
'The Switchblade Kid'

THE NIGHT OF 12 February 1976 had descended over Hollywood as Sal Mineo drove home, tired but exhilarated from rehearsing a new play he was directing. It had the rather ominous title of *PS Your Cat Is Dead*. If he had been superstitious, he might have been unnerved by the death aspect, since his film career had begun to falter after 1965 when he made a picture called *Who Killed Teddy Bear?*

He was thirty-seven, yet still possessed the same dark eyes, the boyish, swarthy Sicilian good looks that had made him an international heart-throb twenty years earlier. Much had changed in his life since those heady days as a movie star when he had made a few million dollars playing young toughs in leather jackets in movies like *Rebel Without a Cause*. His screen persona earned him the tag 'The Switchblade Kid'. In those days he couldn't walk the streets without being mobbed by girls. He'd once boasted, 'I'm not doing bad for the son of a Sicilian coffin-maker from the Bronx.'

Now he wasn't doing so great. The adulation had long passed, the millions he'd made were spent and his acting career was all but over. But he wasn't down and out. He had directed a number of stage productions and had plans to direct a movie. He wasn't broke, but he wasn't rolling in it either. He had sold his Hollywood house six years previously and now lived alone in a small $75 a month Hollywood apartment.

At least he was working, and it thrilled him to know that his new play would open next week in Los Angeles. He lived in the hope that it would lead to something bigger, something better. He had lived in that hope for five years.

He pulled into the car park behind his apartment block. He left his car and headed down the dark, deserted alley that would take him to the entrance of the building. From the shadows someone watched him.

160

Residents of the block were suddenly shaken by a stark scream and the voice of Mineo crying, 'My God, my God, help me.' Then they heard a final scream. And then silence.

They rushed from their homes into the alley. Someone caught sight of a man with blond hair running away. Then they found Sal Mineo, blood gushing from a hole in his chest. The Switchblade Kid had been stabbed to death.

Panic swept over Hollywood at the news of Mineo's death. It was the same tide of fear that had gripped the rich and famous of Los Angeles seven years earlier following the Sharon Tate massacre by the Manson 'family'. Once again movie and music stars were loading their guns, unleashing the guard dogs and hiring bodyguards. If there was a maniac loose in Los Angeles whose prime targets were the stars, nobody was taking any chances.

The police were unable to calm the troubled community. Arriving quickly on the scene, they examined the body and questioned a number of willing witnesses. Some had seen a young man with long, blond hair running away as they raced out into the alley after hearing Mineo's cry for help. There was no apparent motive for the killing. Nothing had been taken from Mineo's body.

But there was one theory which quickly came to detectives' minds. Mineo had been taking a keen interest in prison reform and had befriended a number of ex-cons. There was a distinct possibility that Mineo's killer might have been one of the very people he had been helping to reform. That Sal Mineo should have been involved in such a worthy and charitable enterprise should not have been too surprising. He had himself once been on the wrong side of the law in his early years and had undergone a successful reformation programme that had led him into show business.

He had been born Salvatore Mineo on 10 January 1939 in Harlem in New York to parents who were Sicilian immigrants. His father made coffins. For most of his childhood years, Sal was brought up in the tough Bronx neighbourhoods and quickly learned how to take care of himself. Even as a child he couldn't keep out of trouble, and at the age of eight he was expelled from school and spent the rest of his childhood years in special schools. When he was ten he was forced into a dancing class and before long he was being pushed into school plays. He began to acquire a taste for acting and he developed his talents.

As in the best of all Hollywood traditions, a casting director saw him in a school play, liked him and landed him a role in a stage production of Tennessee Williams's *The Rose Tattoo* opposite Eli Wallach and Maureen Stapleton. In 1952 he made his Broadway debut as the young prince in *The King and I*, enjoying a two-year run with Yul Brynner. Then Hollywood beckoned and in 1955 Sal played featured roles in *Six Bridges to Cross* with Tony Curtis, *The Private War of Major Benson* with Charlton Heston and then two films with James Dean – *Rebel Without a Cause* for which Sal was nominated for an Oscar, and *Giant*. In just one year Mineo had achieved international fame and an Oscar nomination. He also, in that same year, was nominated for an Emmy for his performance in a TV production, *Dino*.

It was an auspicious beginning for Mineo who went on to star in *Exodus*, for which he was nominated again, *The Longest Day*, *Cheyenne Autumn* and a host of other important pictures. Sal always credited his reformation from a life of crime to the efforts of those who recognized his talents and steered him in the right direction. His rehabilitation had been complete.

Or had it?

As detectives pursued their investigation of Sal Mineo's death, they picked up a lead that led them to suspect that Mineo may well have been the victim of a swindled drugs dealer. It was a theory which caused even greater panic among certain members of the Hollywood community. If there was any truth in this latest suggestion by detectives, then there were a great number of people who had good cause to fear retribution.

Cocaine was Hollywood's favourite narcotic. It was very much a status symbol during the late Nineteen-seventies. Too often, people measured anyone's success by the quantity and quality of the expensive drug that was handed around in social circles. In 1976 it cost around $50 a gram. It was important for some who were perhaps no longer the toast of the town to attempt to keep up appearances, and that could well mean getting into debt with the drug peddlers and failing to pay up.

Police knew that Sal Mineo was not living high and dry. He was fighting to perpetuate his career as a director and times were comparatively lean.

There had been a time in the late Fifties when Sal Mineo had been the hottest property around. He received thousands of letters each week from adoring girls. Once, when his car was spotted outside a Beverly Hills health club, a horde of screaming teenagers invaded the building and made off with his clothes.

At the height of his fame he was the leader of a sort of junior 'Rat Pack', modelled after Sinatra's famous pack of cronies. Included were British actress Jill Haworth, Portland Mason (daughter of James Mason) and the daughter of Rita Hayworth and Aly Khan, Yasmin.

Then, in the mid-Sixties, it was suddenly over. Sal Mineo had cooled. He said:

All of a sudden my agents told me, 'You're not a hot property any more.' And they were right. I wasn't. I wasn't getting too many offers.

There was this whole new craze, 'Let's get new faces.' And all of a sudden all of the good roles I wanted went to the new faces. It got really frustrating. You work so hard to make a name for yourself and suddenly it doesn't count.

When I was getting the offers, they were just more than I could handle. And then when things started to cool off, I couldn't get anything I wanted. The roles I wanted most – in *In Cold Blood* and *The Godfather* – went to new people. My agents were frank with me. I don't dig the salesmanship thing of 'Stick around, baby, it's going to be cool', because it's not going to be cool. When I saw that I wasn't getting offered good roles, I knew things weren't going to get any better.

Many stars who began their movie careers knowing that they would one day come to an end found wise ways to invest their money, but for someone as young as Sal was when he started in pictures, there was only one thing to do with all that beautiful money:

> I made millions – not one million but a few million – but I spent it freely. I spent it, and I don't regret it. I feel that I knew how to live. I enjoyed those years from the time I started making money until I lost it. I had expensive cars, I had a big home in Beverly Hills, I sent my sister and two brothers through college.
>
> I gave fabulous parties to which I invited fabulous people. When you have the facilities and the money, you can meet the kind of people you want to be with, and the communion of these people – great artists and great writers – generates so much excitement. That's not saying they'll come only because you have money, but in order to entertain the way you want to entertain, you have to be in a position to do so.
>
> I look back on all that without regrets. I was happy. A lot of people I know who have a lot of money don't know how to spend it. They don't know how to live to achieve happiness. I was living the way I wanted to do. And then I ceased being a hot property.

Falling out of luck and with funds running out, Mineo caught a plane to Las Vegas for the weekend and gambled what little he had on roulette. He had a specific routine. It entailed buying a round ticket to Vegas so that he could only stay for the weekend. He gambled between nine and twelve hours a day. Whether he was winning or losing, when the time was up he flew back to Los Angeles. When playing roulette he hoped to build up a pot and then go for *chemin de fer*. On this particular weekend, he went specifically to try to win enough to buy him an option on a play he wanted to direct – *Fortune and Men's Eyes*. He needed a thousand dollars. At the end of the weekend he came home with the money he needed and consequently he directed *Fortune and Men's Eyes*.

It was a rather sensational play about homesexuals, although it was never explicit. It proved a tremendous success for Mineo, first on the West Coast and then on Broadway. Then he waited for the Hollywood and Broadway producers to come knocking on his door begging him to direct their films or plays. But no one came knocking. Times became lean again, and he took off to Las Vegas periodically to gamble what funds he had, always sticking to his routine and usually coming out on top. But it didn't solve all his problems.

In 1970 with little prospects of any worthwhile acting or directing jobs – except for a part in *Escape From The Planet of the Apes* as a chimpanzee – he sold his big house and flashy car and headed for London where he hoped to put into operation his plans to produce and direct a film called *The Wrong People*. Things were looking good for a while and preparations went ahead to film in Morocco. But then the Moroccan Government got wind of the film, which involved prostitution and drug trafficking, and they banned Mineo from making it there.

He approached Israel for their assistance, and while things progressed in that area, he flew back to New York to produce a play, *The Children's Mass*. It flopped and closed within a month. Failing to get his film off the ground, Sal returned to Los Angeles where he began renting his apartment for $75 a month, and made plans for the future. But it looked bleak, and as detectives investigated his murder, they couldn't help but take into consideration that Mineo would have had to upgrade his status in business and social circles, and that he was not in a financial situation to meet all the requirements. And so they pursued their drugs theory. However, it led to dead-ends and before long it was dropped.

Following up on the flimsy theories that they had and in the hope of securing more solid evidence, the police entered Mineo's apartment and conducted a search for clues. What they discovered astonished every one of them who remembered the teenage heart-throb.

On the walls hung photographs of nudes. Not nude women, but men. Among them was a picture of a man they identified as a close friend of Mineo's wearing female underwear. Also stashed away was a pile of magazines featuring naked men and blatantly homosexual books. The emphasis of the investigation suddenly shifted dramatically. Police now had to consider that

Sal Mineo was not the straight girl-hungry Casanova who had once boasted, 'My hobby is girls'.

They were now looking, they believed, for a possible jilted lover – the young man with the long, blond hair, perhaps! One detective made the public statement, 'The motive appears to have been jealousy, or revenge, over some personal relationship.'

On 14 February, police began calling at the homes of all known homosexuals in the film colony, searching for the blond youth or for anyone willing to reveal what they knew about Mineo's private life. But was Mineo really gay?

When news broke that he had been murdered, actress Jill Haworth tearfully told the press that he had been her first lover. They had met on the set of the epic *Exodus*. She was just fifteen and making her film debut. He was a handsome, olive-skinned, twenty-year-old movie star with a dozen pictures to his credit. They were together constantly and began a romance that lasted for almost thirteen years on and off. They even got engaged at one point, but broke it off. Said Mineo:

I love Jill. I always will, but I'm not for marriage and kids. I've been on my own since I was about fifteen, and I can't adjust to the responsibility of one person. I've tried it a number of times – I mean, living with someone – and it just hasn't worked out. Jill and I have incredible feelings for each other, but to get married is another thing. The idea of settling down goes against my make-up. What I need is totally different. I need companionship, I need love and all the things that go with it, but I don't need the responsibility of married life. I like my freedom too much.

The general image of Sal Mineo was of a confirmed bachelor, and he naturally perpetuated that image. But there appears to be underneath it all something else that he wasn't prepared to be totally open about. In 1972, talking about his relationship with Jill, he said:

I've chosen my life style over marriage. Jill and I are apart right now. She's in New York. To be honest, I'm sometimes alone and sometimes I have felt terribly lonely, but that's the price I pay. What I'm really saying is that I've found a life style that is much more satisfying in total to me than complete commitment to one person. I really do dig the freedom – always have.

It certainly seems unlikely that Mineo was a practising homosexual in his earlier years, especially during his initial romance with Jill Haworth. But had the loneliness he'd later experienced when things looked bleak led him to seek comfort and companionship in other areas? The first play he directed was about homosexuals – was that the beginning of his secret life? Sal Mineo had certainly expressed, if only privately, homosexual tendencies – tendencies that may have been purely latent and born of desperation. The evidence lies in the pictures and books, all of a homosexual nature, that were discovered in his apartment. They had to belong to him, because he lived alone.

But was this somewhat sad revelation of any importance in the investigation of his murder? Initially, the police thought so, but like the drugs lead it led nowhere, and it seemed for a time at least as though the murder of Sal Mineo would never be solved.

In his early years as a movie idol, Sal Mineo couldn't make a move without it being reported in the gossip columns. By 1976 he couldn't get a mention in a single paragraph. Perhaps he wanted it that way – perhaps he liked his privacy. But the problem was, his privacy turned to solitude. A newspaper headline had once called him the 'Teenager's Dream Boat'. In the end he became something of a sad, emotionally pale imitation of his former self. Just to land a job on a local Los Angeles radio show was enough to excite him. Or so he said. When a fan magazine caught up with him just a few years before his death to find out whatever had happened to Sal Mineo, he talked about the radio show as if it was a big new movie. His 'other exciting projects' included the picture he planned to direct in Israel which never came to anything, and a screenplay he was writing in the hope of selling it to a producer. But then, just about every actor writes at least one screenplay in their lives, and very few indeed ever see them reach the screen.

Sal Mineo ended life living in hope and full of optimism, but underneath his enthusiasm there seemed to beat a fading pulse. One thing that did have a big effect on his last years was the death of his father. He said:

I spent the last five days of my father's life with him in New York, and what I learned from him in those five days was how important the moments are every day and how quickly time goes. Being in the same room with him and looking at him – I realized that one day I would be in the same position as he, facing death. Before it happens I want to do the things I want to do. I don't want to end up saying, 'I wish I had.'

He died before he was ready, before he had done the things he wanted to. And what he wanted to do was to be *someone* again. Yet it was only after he was found knifed to death in a dark alley that his name became a household word again, simply because of such pitiful headlines as SWITCHBLADE KID KNIFING HAUNTS FILMLAND and GAYS FACE QUIZ OVER MINEO'S MURDER.

It wasn't until two years later that police managed to link his murder to a young convict, twenty-one-year-old Lionel Williams. He was actually in prison, convicted of forgery, when just four days from the end of his prison term, on 5 January 1978, Williams was charged with Mineo's murder. After all the unpleasant background to Mineo's life that had been dug up simply through the police investigation into his death, it turned out that the police department's first theory was correct. Mineo had been killed by one of the very people he had been trying to help. Consequently, Williams wasn't released from prison but was found guilty of the first-degree murder of Sal Mineo and sentenced to life imprisonment. Yet as sad and as tragic as the death of Sal Mineo was, the greatest sadness is that Hollywood turned its back on a great talent, not allowing him to reach his full potential as an actor during his short life.

CASE 13
Gig Young: Game of Death

IT WASN'T SURPRISING that Hollywood actor and Oscar winner Gig Young preferred to have his groceries delivered to his Manhattan apartment. He was still honeymooning with his bride of three weeks, German actress Kim Schmidt. Everyone agreed that they'd never known Gig to be so happy. For the gaunt-looking, grey-haired actor of sixty-four, taking a beautiful, healthy bride of thirty-one could have been a sign that he was trying to overcome some of the problems he had been plagued with for so long. Too much alcohol had taken a terrible toll of him, and eight years earlier he had suffered a heart attack that had robbed him of his good, meaty looks and and left him drawn and frail. He'd also had to overcome skin cancer.

It was natural that he wanted to be alone with his new wife. And besides, few actors dared to go out on to the streets, especially in New York. It was October 1978, and the killer of Sal Mineo had not yet been found. No movie star felt safe, and Young could well afford to pay for his groceries to be delivered. He wasn't a wealthy film star. In fact, he'd worked very little since his coronary, but he'd earned a nice fee recently starring in the hastily restructured kung-fu flick, *The Game of Death* which Bruce Lee had begun to make when he suddenly died a few years earlier. In fact, Gig had met Kim while making *Game of Death* the previous year in Hong Kong. And everyone agreed that they made a very happy couple.

Then, one sad day in mid-October 1978, the sound of a gunshot echoed through the Manhattan apartment block. A second shot quickly followed. No one dared to investigate. Violence and crime were rife in New York and people preferred to keep themselves to themselves. They didn't want to get involved. If people wanted security they should make sure that their doors and windows were tightly locked, and if people were foolish enough not to do so, then they practically invited intruders packing firearms. So nobody in the block went to investigate the sound of gunshots.

169

Throughout the day numerous delivery boys with grocery bags had come to Gig Young's door, but when Young failed to respond to their call, they simply left the bags to pile up outside in the corridor. It was only when a passing neighbour noticed the pile of grocery bags that curiosity was finally aroused. The neighbour tried to summon Gig Young, but there was no answer. Becoming alarmed, he called for the police.

They broke in and found two bodies lying face down on the floor of the bedroom. One was of Kim, a bullet in her head; the other was of Gig Young, who had been shot through the mouth. A pistol was still tightly grasped in his hand.

On a desk in the bedroom was a diary, opened at 27 September 1978. It read: 'We got married today.'

Sergeant Thomas Fahey of the New York Police was given the task of fending off the press who swarmed round the apartment block as soon as they got wind of the shooting.

'It looks like murder-suicide,' he announced to the reporters. 'There was no note, but we are talking to friends and relatives and hope to find out whether Mr Young was under any kind of pressure. At this stage, we don't think anyone else is involved.'

It made for sensational headlines: GIG YOUNG KILLS HIS BRIDE AND HIMSELF. Certainly suicide among movie actors was nothing new, but for an actor of Gig Young's calibre and standing to kill his own wife before taking his own life was unprecedented in the history of Hollywood. It was also, for his friends and family, a total shock. In Hollywood he was regarded not only as a fine actor but a very good friend to many celebrities. He was easily liked and made no enemies. But even more surprising, no one was even vaguely aware of any kind of worry or pressure Young was under that could have driven him to such a desperate act.

The police investigation did nothing to dig beneath the happy-go-lucky personality that everyone knew and liked. He'd possessed an immediately likeable character ever since he first arrived in Hollywood in 1940 playing bit parts in movies under his own name, Byron Elsworth Barr. By coincidence there was another actor called Byron Barr, but that was the name Gig had been given when he was born in St Cloud, Minnesota on 4 November 1913.

He'd been raised in Washington, DC, where he began acting in high school plays. After graduating, he worked nights in an amateur theatrical company and days in an automobile agency. He gained a scholarship to the Pasadena Playhouse where his work led to a contract with Warner Bros. in 1940. He played several walk-on parts before landing his first leading role in *The Gay Sisters* in 1942. In that film, he played a character by the name of Gig Young. Because of the confusion between him and the other Byron Barr, he adopted the name of Gig Young.

His movie career was interrupted by the war and he served with the Coast Guard until 1947, when he returned to Hollywood and freelanced successfully, landing roles that usually cast him in second leads in major movies such as *The Three Musketeers* with Gene Kelly and Lana Turner, and *Wake of the Red Witch* supporting John Wayne. But occasionally he got the lead role in B pictures.

He was considered a very capable, dependable and versatile actor. The light-hearted amiability that he projected in most of his roles was part of himself, and earned him many friends. His career was given a huge boost in 1951 when he was cast in *Come Fill the Cup* for which he was nominated for an Oscar as Best Supporting Actor. Seven years later he was nominated in the same category for the comedy *Teacher's Pet*. He finally won the Oscar as Best Supporting Actor for *They Shoot Horses, Don't They?*, made in 1969. It was the culmination of his career, proving, perhaps, that Gig Young was a stalwart supporting player, but not quite strong enough to succeed as a leading man.

It was shortly after appearing in *They Shoot Horses, Don't They?* that Gig had a heart attack. By the time he collected his Oscar at the 1970 Academy Awards show, he was suddenly a much older man, looking decidedly more aged than his fifty-six years. His film work began to be less frequent. He made *Lovers and Other Strangers* in 1970, but then dropped out of the scene for four years, re-emerging in Sam Peckinpah's *Bring Me the Head of Alfredo Garcia*. A couple more films followed in 1975 and then came another few idle years. Finally, in 1978, he landed a lead role in *The Game of Death* with a Bruce Lee look-alike, utilizing the few martial arts sequences that Lee had actually shot in 1973 before he died so tragically young. The producers, eager to complete the film, managed to rewrite the script, hire a cast including Gig Young, and actually get it into release in 1979 after Young's death. The film was hardly a fitting tribute to the talents of either Bruce Lee or Gig Young.

It was while on location in Hong Kong that Gig met and fell in love with German actress Kim Schmidt. On 27 September, they were married in New York. He had been married three times before. His third wife had been Elizabeth Montgomery, who played the lovable witch Samantha in the TV series 'Bewitched'. Young's fourth marriage at the age of sixty-four to the lovely blonde German girl seemed to give him a new lease of life. But his health was poor and he had a long-standing drink problem. However, these did not seem to be things that bothered Gig during those three weeks of marriage to Kim. Only days before the tragedy, friends had seen Gig and Kim happily kissing and hugging in a restaurant. Police had, of course, considered that on the fateful day Gig and Kim may have engaged in a violent row that had led to their deaths, but they could determine nothing to strengthen that theory from those who testified of the newly-weds' behaviour during the week before they died.

Gig's agent Martin Baum told police, 'He seemed like a man who had everything going for him. How little we know.'

Young's business agent, Ed Trauber, told police that he had spoken to Gig on the phone just days before he died. 'He sounded fine,' said Trauber. 'There seemed to be no problem.'

The police had no doubt that Gig Young had shot his wife and then put the gun to his own mouth. But they were unable to find any motive, and that left the death of Gig Young shrouded in mystery with no one able to help those who liked and loved him to understand how such a gentle and amiable man could suddenly turn murderer, killing the woman he loved after just three weeks of marriage. The case was left open, subject to sordid speculation.

And then, two days after the discovery of Young and his wife dead in their apartment, a mysterious woman entered the scene and put a whole new slant on the tragedy.

Harriette Douglas was fifty-eight. She had flown in from California with, she said, permission from Gig Young's sister to make the funeral arrangements. What she had to say regarding her relationship with Gig Young was of great interest to the police.

They allowed her to identify the body of the dead actor at the morgue after hearing her incredible story. According to this woman, who insisted she was a 'Mrs', she and Gig had been lovers for the past ten years. Theirs had been a rather secretive affair that only a few close friends and family knew about. They shared a home in Los Angeles which was in his name.

Then, in 1978, he became besotted with this young actress from Germany, Kim Schmidt, while making a movie in Hong Kong. Harriette begged him, 'Don't marry her. If you must, take her to New York. Live with her and get it over with. But don't marry her.'

'Look,' said Gig, 'let's not let any crazy things I do spoil our relationship.'

Young went ahead and married Kim, leaving Mrs Douglas to make arrangements to sell his house in California. Although happy with his new bride, Gig wanted to stay in touch with Harriette. She told him, 'Never phone me behind your wife's back. If you must call me, keep everything out in the open.'

Harriette was very anxious for Gig. She knew, and had dealt with, his drink problem. She was concerned that Kim wouldn't be able to handle Gig if he started drinking heavily or even taking pills. Mrs Douglas telephoned Kim and told her not to let him drink at all or to take any kind of pills.

Only a week before the tragedy, Harriette had called Gig to discuss his will. She told police, 'He left a will that was signed with me in it. But there was a will, not signed, that left me out.'

When she learned that Gig and Kim were dead, she made hasty arrangements with members of Gig's family to sort out the funeral and make the formal identification.

Police were satisfied with her story which, she said, she told because 'I want him remembered with dignity and not as a murderer.'

Mrs Douglas's story certainly posed some new questions. Had Gig been drinking or taking pills, leading to a violent confrontation between himself and his bride? Or had there been cross words concerning the mystery lover, Mrs Harriette Douglas?

Or had Gig Young simply had enough of life and, against Harriette's advice, gone ahead and married a young bride, knowing full well that he would soon end his life, intending to finish it happily? What is certain is that beneath the devil-may-care façade that his agents and friends saw was a soul in anguish and torment, probably caused by his troubled love life, possibly due to his drink and health problems and maybe even attributable to emotional and mental disturbances.

Although the police were sure that Young had killed his wife, his memory remains one of a versatile actor who won the coveted Oscar, rather than that of a killer. In fact, such was his warm, amiable personality that no one who knew, or knew of him, considers him anything less than a fine man and an accomplished actor who died under the most tragic of circumstances.

Murder in Hollywood

NOT SURPRISINGLY, MANY of today's Hollywood stars live in fear. When John Lennon was gunned down right outside his apartment block in New York in December 1980 by Mark David Chapman, it sent shock waves vibrating through the entertainment industry. Chapman had been a fan who, only a week earlier, had actually asked for and received an autograph from Lennon. Celebrities were now always at risk from their fans.

The risk had once been more from within showbiz society than from without. It was once the powers that presided over the rich and famous who virtually decided the outcome of any such crime – today it seems inconceivable to us that the men who made movies – men like Adolph Zukor and possibly William Randolph Hearst – could wield such power and authority as to override even the law. But those 'halcyon' days of silent movies were still early days for law enforcement in and around Hollywood. As columnist Adela Rogers St Johns has said, Hollywood in those days was 'the wild and woolly west'.

As the law strengthened, so did organized crime, bringing fear and death to places like Beverly Hills. Even the motion picture business itself was infiltrated by people with strong gangster connections – people such as George Raft and Virginia Hill. But if movie stars and film-makers felt that there was a constant threat from those who broke the law, they couldn't guarantee that they were any safer when the men who ran the country began moving in Hollywood circles. Finally, the violence that was breeding rapidly in the streets of America became an ever-constant threat to the movie colony.

This was, of course, brought home forcefully following the murders of Ramon Novarro, Sharon Tate and Sal Mineo. Another victim was former MGM director Robert B. Sinclair. One night in 1970 an intruder broke into his home and stabbed Sinclair to death while his actress wife, Heather Angel, watched helplessly.

No wonder Hollywood has become a community of houses as secure as Fort Knox. The very latest and most elaborate intruder-proof systems are in regular use. Warren Beatty went so far as to instal a kidnap-proof vault. And if that sounds more like a case of pure paranoia, it has been fostered only by the increase in kidnap threats and extortion in Los Angeles over the past decade with many movie stars as potential targets.

Charlie's Angel Jaclyn Smith has had a number of harrowing encounters with strangers, prompting her to buy an extra guard dog to keep at her side. Most film and TV folk now have a gun of some kind in their homes as a matter of course. Defence has become a way of life and this can come as quite a culture shock for newcomers to Hollywood society. British actress Susan George told me how she refused to have a gun in her house when she first arrived in Hollywood. Everyone urged her to get one, offering to give her firearms training. But she was quite unaware of the danger that she might find herself in until one day she heard a woman screaming hysterically on her doorstep.

'My attitude was always not to leave a screaming woman out in the street,' said Susan, 'so I let her in and called the police. They took her away, but the officer said to me, "You must be crazy. Don't you ever let someone like this in your house again. This woman might have killed you." '

No wonder old residents of Hollywood have gone to great lengths to make sure that no one could possibly so much as scream on their doorstep. Most houses have high walls and remote-controlled gates. Sometimes there's even a polite warning, such as the sign that hangs by the gates of Sinatra's Beverly Hills home. It reads, 'If you ring this bell, you better have a damned good reason.' You can almost hear the unwritten 'or else!'

Perhaps it was inevitable that eventually the movie stars would start moving out of Hollywood altogether, seeking peace and solitude usually in the country or, in Robert Redford's case, up in the mountains of Utah. Actually, Redford has lived on his remote mountain top near Provo, Utah, since 1964 when he was still only a new face on the screen. Now a millionaire movie idol, he prefers to remain far away from the trappings of Hollywood and stay close to his own skiing resort, appropriately called The Sundance Ski Resort.

Even an old hellraiser like Lee Marvin prefers to live out in the middle of nowhere. These days he's perfectly settled at his remote home near Tucson in Arizona. But for most of America's TV and movie personnel Hollywood is still home and for them living behind locked gates, high walls and in grounds patrolled by ferocious guard dogs is just a way of life. Or more a way of keeping death at bay. But then, not even such elaborate defence systems always guarantee peace of mind or escape from threats.

Death threats against film and TV stars have become more frequent in recent years. At first the police didn't take too much notice of them, as with the case of British actress Jane Seymour. It was while still a newcomer to Hollywood in 1979 and starring in the TV sci-fi series 'Battlestar Galactica' that Jane began receiving terrifying death threats.

It started with a series of peculiar telegrams arriving at the homes of Jane's agent and people she was working with at the time. There was nothing really threatening about them then, but Jane was convinced someone was trying to hassle her. She tried to ignore them, but then one day she received a telegram at her home which said that she would be killed that weekend. The following morning her agent received an anonymous telephone call from someone who claimed that he had been paid to kill her. That's when she decided to call in the police.

Initially the FBI took an interest in the case but finally handed it over to the Beverly Hills police. Jane was told by the police that even if they knew who was making these threats there was nothing they could do unless she was physically attacked. As she wisely noted at the time, 'Once a physical attack happens, it would be too late.'

It didn't help her peace of mind that she didn't know why she was being threatened. She could only guess that someone didn't want her working in Hollywood. She'd been very busy since arriving there and she reasoned, 'It could well be someone who is jealous of me. It could be because I've worked a lot since I've been here and somebody doesn't like that. What other reason could there be?'

She never found out because, sensibly, she moved house and for a time her address was kept secret. The threats ceased and since then, thank goodness, she has been left alone and unharmed.

Being public figures, actors all too often have to put aside any fears they might have, since many of them still work in the theatre where they are exposed to the public and, occasionally, to danger. In 1981 Jodie Foster performed in a play while a maniac who had sworn to kill her sat in the audience. It happened during her absence from movies to study at Yale University. She was in a college play, and through two performances twenty-two-year-old Edward Richardson watched her. In his pocket was a loaded pistol. Jodie remained blissfully unaware of the danger until Richardson was arrested by police.

The call had gone out for him following the discovery in his hotel room by a maid of a parcel addressed to Jodie Foster. It contained a letter in which he said he would kill her and President Reagan. Only a week earlier the movie-star-turned-President-of-the-United-States had been wounded in an assassination attempt by John Hinkley. Richardson said in his letter that he would 'bring to completion Hinkley's reality' and kill Reagan. Also enclosed was a photograph of Reagan with a huge X drawn across it. It was marked, 'Targeted for death'.

Continuing the letter, Richardson wrote that he would kill her as well as 'finish what Hinkley started. RR [Reagan] must die. JWH [Hinkley] has told me in a prophetic dream. You too will suffer the same fate as Reagan and others in this fascist regime. You cannot escape. We are a wave of assassins throughout the world.'

Upon discovery of the parcel, an alert went out and Richardson was picked up at a New York bus depot with a loaded gun in his pocket. He was clearly a crank, but the police were quite convinced that he intended to carry out his threats, although they did rule out any connection between him and Hinkley who, like Richardson, had an obsession with Jodie Foster.

At least Jodie Foster hadn't actually come face to face with a killer, unlike Farrah Fawcett who did while in a play in 1983. She was starring in *Extremities* in New York, and had just come to the end of a rape scene when a man leaped on to the stage brandishing a sharp metal instrument. He began ranting at her, but she tried to ignore him and just carry on with the play.

'I'm talking to you,' he shouted, waving the weapon at her. 'I've been looking for you. I love you! I love you!'

The audience simply took it to be part of the play, but the terror on Farrah's face was real. That old saying that the show must go on was certainly adhered to that night as all the actors on stage did their best to continue reciting their lines. No one at that moment had any idea just how dangerous a situation it was, especially for Farrah. The maniac continued ranting. 'I'm from the US Marines and I wrote you a letter. Why haven't you answered my letter?'

Farrah was now in tears and at last sensing there was real danger to their leading lady, stage hands pounced on the maniac and led him away to be arrested by police. He gave his name as Arnold DeGennare. They charged him with disorderly conduct and then released him. It proved to be a big mistake. Police only later discovered that DeGennare had just been released from prison after serving a mere six years for murder. An immediate call went out to find and apprehend DeGennare and police thereafter kept a close watch on Farrah Fawcett who, at the time of her confrontation, had had no idea that she had just come face to face with a killer.

More often than not, death threats arrive at movie stars' homes totally anonymously, and it's difficult to know whether or not to take them seriously. Walter Matthau certainly did take things seriously in 1979 when he received a letter demanding around $150,000 or his son Charles would be killed. Matthau told the police and, in this particular case, they put a round-the-clock watch on Charles Matthau. They even managed to catch the culprit, an eighteen-year-old student.

Charlton Heston also took the death threats he received in 1984 seriously. These followed a controversy Heston had become involved in within the Screen Actors Guild. He deeply opposed a move by the SAG president, *Lou Grant's* Ed Asner, to merge with the Screen Extras Guild. At the time there was also controversy over remarks Asner had made about El Salvador. During one meeting there was a heated exchange between Heston and Asner who accused the epic-proportioned star of *Dynasty II The Colbys* of fostering a 'master race mentality among performers'. Heston demanded an apology, contending that the 'master race' remark branded him a Nazi. Asner refused.

After that Heston received some death threats, prompting him to write, 'clearly Mr. Asner's radical allegiances and El Salvadorian rebel enthusiasms trigger the adrenalin in the extreme fringe of his supporters'. The police took an interest in the matter and kept a more than usually diligent watch on Heston and his family. Fortunately, the threats amounted to nothing more.

Such threats to *Rambo* star Sylvester Stallone, however, did start turning into a reality. Late in 1985, while Stallone was filming *Cobra* in Mexico, a plague of death threats was followed by the planting of a deadly snake in his bed in the villa he was renting. Consequently, the producers hired a veritable army of security men to watch Stallone's every move, and the police also investigated the matter.

Several years ago Marie Osmond received threats upon her life when the Osmonds were recording their TV shows in Hollywood. But where were the police then? The Osmond family had no recourse but to flee Hollywood and set up their own studio in their home town of Provo, Utah. Like Jane Seymour, Marie Osmond was not accorded police protection, and safety was only ensured by getting out while the going was good. Perhaps it's only in recent years when death threats to stars have become more frequent that police have learned not to take such menacing warnings lightly.

Perhaps ironically, though just as tragically, the most common threat to the lives of stars comes from their own selves. Suicide, which many regard as self-murder, accounts for more deaths among people in the film and television world, than death at the hands of others. There are perhaps exceptions, but in nearly all cases of suicide in Hollywood, the real killer has been an intangible creature called stardom which comes and goes too quickly for many. Stardom is a peculiar phenomenon which picks people up, sometimes from nowhere, and puts them right at the top from where there is nowhere else to go but down. The trappings of stardom all too often are too much for the idols of millions to bear losing when fame and popularity start to wane. Unable to face life as has-beens, a harrowing number of actors, actresses and occasionally even those behind the cameras have taken their own lives.

Never in the history of Hollywood was there such a tidal wave of self-murders than that which followed the coming of sound to motion pictures. There were many who had been able to set the box-office tills ringing in film after film during the silent era, but when they had to start talking the audience stayed away in droves. Among these can be counted Karl Dane who shot to prominence in *The Big Parade* in 1925. A has-been by the age of forty-eight, he shot himself in 1934 having gone from being a major movie star to a hot-dog salesman in just a year. There was also John Bowers who'd been in pictures since 1916. But after the advent of sound he couldn't even get a walk-on part. Depressed and broke, he walked naked into the Pacific and drowned in 1936. Lou Tellegen had been a sophisticated leading man in silent films. His career came to an end following the new era of talking pictures, and he stabbed himself with a pair of scissors and died surrounded by scrapbooks containing his press cuttings. Other stars who couldn't take the fall from grace because of their inability to make the transition to the talking screen were Milton Sills who deliberately drove his car over a cliff; Robert Ames who gassed himself; and Jeanne Eagels who died from an overdose of heroin.

One could add to that list the names of many who took their own lives after sound became firmly established – Pedro Armendariz, friend and often co-star of John Wayne, shot himself in 1963 while dying of cancer, aged fifty-one; Scotty Beckett, a member of the 'Our Gang' kids slashed his wrists in 1960, survived and took a fatal overdose in 1968, aged thirty-eight; Carole Landis, star of *One Million B.C.* overdosed on sleeping pills in 1948, aged twenty-nine; Chester Morris, star of silents and early talkies, took an overdose of barbiturates in 1970 aged sixty-nine while suffering from stomach cancer; Margaret

Sullavan, highly acclaimed actress of the Thirties and Forties, overdosed on sleeping pills on New Year's Day 1960, aged forty-nine; Charles Boyer, veteran French heart-throb, killed himself with Seconal in 1978, aged eighty-one, just two days after his beloved wife Pat Paterson died of cancer; James Murray, star of the silent classic *The Crowd* and a chronic alcoholic, leapt to his death in the Hudson River in 1936, aged thirty-five; Trent Lehman, child star of TV's *Nanny and the Professor*, hanged himself in 1982 aged twenty; Claire Maynard, teenage starlet with Fox in the Thirties, gassed herself in 1941; Grant Withers, a favourite actor of John Ford, overdosed on sleeping pills in 1959, aged fifty-five; Clara Blandick, famous as Aunt Em in *The Wizard of Oz*, ended the misery of arthritic pain by taking sleeping pills in 1962, aged eighty-one; James Cardwell, star of *A Walk in the Sun*, shot himself in 1954, aged thirty-three; Barbara Bates, who made her debut in *Salome Where She Danced*, gassed herself in 1969, aged forty-four; Pier Angeli, lovely Italian-born star who faded in the Sixties, overdosed on barbiturates in 1971, aged thirty-nine; Lupe Valez, the 'Mexican Spitfire', swallowed Seconal in 1944, aged thirty-six; George Sanders, suave Russian-born star of American and British films, swallowed five tubes of Nembutal in 1972, aged sixty-five; Ona Munson, Belle Watling in *Gone with the Wind*, took barbiturates in 1955, aged forty-nine; Ross Alexander, Jeremy Pitt opposite Errol Flynn's Captain Blood, shot himself in 1937, aged twenty-nine; Albert Dekker, famous as Dr Cyclops, hanged himself in 1968, aged sixty-four; George Reeves, TV's Superman in the Fifties, shot himself in 1959, aged forty-five; Maggie McNamara, star of *Three Coins in the Fountain* and *The Moon Is Blue*, had a history of mental illness and overdosed on sleeping pills in 1978, aged forty-nine; Gail Russell, star of numerous supernatural films of the Forties, attempted suicide several times and succeeded in 1961, mixing liquor and barbiturates, aged thirty-six; Jean Seberg, famous as Saint Joan, attempted suicide numerous times, finally overdosing on barbiturates in 1979, aged forty; Inger Stevens, Swedish-born beauty, attempted suicide in 1959 by swallowing pills and ammonia, and killed herself with barbiturates in 1970, aged thirty-five.

Add to that names of stars who died from possible suicide, such as Alan Ladd, Nick Adams, Gia Scala, Everett Sloane and Dorothy Dandridge, and you begin to realize that movie stardom – or rather the effects of stardom – can be the biggest killer in the movie business.

There are other kinds of killers beside people with knives, guns or poison. They are the kind who kill for profit; yet who are never indicted for murder, or even manslaughter. They are, in the words of victim Alma Rubens, the 'murderers who sell drugs'.

Drug peddlers are rife in and around Hollywood. They service those who need that little extra help in coping with the tremendous pressures that stardom brings. As has been said, there is nothing new about drug abuse among the film colony. Although today's headlines are frequently taken up with news of yet another pop star's demise through drug abuse, down through the decades since movies were first made the number of screen stars who have died hopeless junkies is frighteningly high.

One of Hollywood's first drug dealers was shown as 'The Count'. His true identity is unknown today, but Mack Sennett star Juanita Hansen, one of The Count's best customers, once said, 'The man was really a fairly well-known actor, through not a star.' She should know. She paid $75 for an ounce of heroin from him regularly. She was more fortunate than others who bought drugs from him. She survived to found the Juanita Hansen Foundation to combat drug addiction. But it was too late to save Mabel Normand and Barbara La Marr.

Nothing could be done for Wallace Reid either. He was Paramount's top star when he was suddenly blacklisted following the establishment of Will Hays as the official Hollywood watchdog. Hays had a doom list compiled of all Hollywood personalities whose lifestyles risked scandal. Reid was addicted to morphine which was administered to him by his studio doctors to keep him going following injuries to his head in a train crash. The Count was very quickly in on the scene, keeping Reid high on the stuff until he couldn't do without it.

At Hays's insistence, Paramount had Reid committed to a

private sanatorium in March 1922. He spent the rest of the year in a padded cell, undergoing total withdrawal of his daily dose of morphine. It's said that his 'cold turkey' treatment unhinged his mind, and he died in his cell on 18 January 1923. The rumour was whispered in Hollywood that he had been 'put to sleep'.

Alma Rubens, who began her film career in D.W. Griffith's *Intolerance*, also payed the price of drug abuse when she died aged just thirty-three. Very shortly before her death she revealed that she had begun taking morphine when a doctor prescribed it for some pain she had. 'Take this for the pain,' he had told her, 'and you'll be able to go on.' The pain didn't go away and she took more and more morphine until she was hooked. She went to other doctors, one of whom laughed when she told him that she constantly craved morphine. He told her, 'You won't need any more after you are well.'

But Alma never got well. There is no cure for drug addiction. She eventually moved on to heroin which began to destroy her physically and emotionally. Finally, her physician called for an ambulance to take her to the Alhambra Clinic. As they came to take her, she screamed, 'I'm being kidnapped,' and fled to a nearby gas station. She managed to stab one of the ambulance men but was overpowered when a gas attendant helped out, and she was taken screaming and kicking to the clinic. From there she was sent to the psychiatric ward of LA General Hospital and then on to the California State Hospital for the Insane. But Alma wasn't insane. She was a drug addict, and when she left six months later apparently cured, she was still an addict.

For the next three years she attempted to make a comeback, but in January 1921 she was arrested for possession of morphine. By that time she was dying and was allowed to go home. Heroin had taken its toll on her body, and on 22 January 1921 she died, but not before telling newspapermen about the 'murderers who sell this poison and who escape punishment when caught by buying their way out'.

It isn't always the maniac or the just plain evil man who kills, or attempts to kill, or even simply contemplates killing. Some of Hollywood's most prominent figures have found themselves on charges of manslaughter or attempted murder. And at least one movie idol has confessed to contemplating murder. He is Stewart Granger. His planned target was movie mogul Howard Hughes.

Since the coming of sound to movies, there have been few men in the business more powerful than Howard Hughes. His power was bought by his legendary wealth, and he could be bloody-minded enough to make life hell for anyone. Which is what he did for Stewart Granger and Jean Simmons, then Mrs Granger. She was under contract to Hughes who really was not the most dedicated of film-makers and took little of the personal interest in his stars, as did other studio heads. He treated Jean Simmons with such little regard that she and Granger ultimately took Hughes to litigation. They won, freeing Jean from her contract. But before the case, Granger actually made plans to kill Hughes, such was his hatred for the man. He spent a day and a night just mentally going through the motions of it, but he says, 'when I woke up the next morning I realized it was a silly thing, and changed my mind'.

Perhaps it's often that extra time to think things over that has prevented more than just the one potential killer from killing. Perhaps if producer Walter Wanger had had time to cool down and think things over, he might not have shot and wounded agent Jennings Lang in 1951. The incident occurred when Wanger saw his wife, actress Joan Bennett, with Lang who was her agent, in a parking lot. He had suspected them of having an affair and took this encounter between them to be an arranged meeting for things other than professional matters. In a fit of jealousy, he pulled a gun and fired. He hit Lang in the groin. He was convicted and served several months in prison, spending his term inside as prison librarian. Upon his release he was reunited with his wife, but the marriage was doomed and ended in divorce. As though intending to bow out of his career and his life in one big finale, Wanger masterminded the most disastrous epic in film history, *Cleopatra*, starring Elizabeth Taylor.

The Wanger–Lang incident was reminiscent of another that occurred in 1938 on the doorstep of Ruth Etting, the star of a number of early musicals. Her mobster husband, Martin ('Moe the Gimp') Snyder found her with her lover, pianist Myrl

Alderman, and promptly shot him. Alderman survived and Snyder was charged with attempted murder. During the trial, Etting divorced Snyder and married the pianist.

The arrest of legendary choreographer Buzby Berkeley for second-degree murder in 1935 was a different type of case altogether. It was a charge that stemmed from an incident that occurred right at the height of his success. His musical numbers in Warner Bros. pictures such as *42nd Street* were the envy of every studio. His talent really exploded on the screen when he directed his first complete picture, *Gold Diggers of 1935*. But that was also the year in which his career began to disintegrate following his trial for murder.

The nightmare began on 8 September while Berkeley was driving home from a party given by William Koenig of Warners to mark the completion of filming on *In Caliente*. He'd had too much to drink and he lost control of his car as he sped along the Pacific Coast Highway. Suddenly he was driving down the wrong side of the road straight into oncoming traffic. He rammed head-first into a car, bounced off it and hit another. Three people died in the pile-up, and Berkeley was charged with second-degree murder.

He suffered head and leg injuries and had to be brought into court on a stretcher. His defence was in the hands of Jerry Geisler who produced the blown-out left front tyre from Berkeley's car in an attempt to prove that this was the cause of the fatal accident. The jury were confounded and the trial ended in deadlock. A second trial was held in which seven members of the jury voted for acquittal while the other five held out for a verdict of guilty. A third trial was opened in September 1936. Berkeley, now recovered from his physical injuries, became a nervous wreck, standing trial by day while shooting a movie by night. This time, he was acquitted. He claimed that it was his non-stop work schedule that saved his sanity during the trials, but ten years later he had the nervous breakdown that had been looming over him since the car crash. He slashed his wrists and throat, unable to come to terms with his ailing career, his bad luck and his alcoholism. It was his Japanese houseboy who rescued him from death, bandaging him up and calling for assistance. He had to be subdued by police before he'd allow ambulancemen to cart him off to hospital. He ended up in the psychiatric ward where he spent six horrendous weeks.

Just to prove that there were some moguls with heart, Jack Warner hired him to direct the musical sequences for Doris Day's *Romance on the High Seas* in 1948. He continued to work until he retired after making *Jumbo* in 1962, and died peacefully in 1976.

A similar harrowing tale is told of actress Lynne Baggett, one-time wife of producer Sam Spiegel. She was charged with manslaughter in 1954 when she ran her car into a stationwagon full of boys returning from a summer camp. A nine-year-old boy was killed and four others injured. But Lynne didn't wait around to find that out. She drove on in her smashed-up car, only to be apprehended by police and charged with manslaughter. She was acquitted but was found guilty of hit-and-run driving, serving a fifty-day jail sentence.

A year later Spiegel divorced her and from there her life and career plummeted. In 1959 she tried to kill herself with sleeping pills, but it was in 1960 that she managed to bring her life to an end with an overdose of barbiturates.

Now we've covered all the major Hollywood murder cases, and taken a look at some of the lesser ones. But all are indicative of the topsy-turvy lifestyles, the sometimes intolerable pressure, the almost unreal world of movie-makers where the one great reality that they have in common with the rest of mankind is death. It's just that Hollywood folk seem to meet it more dramatically, more theatrically than the common crowd. But isn't that what Hollywood is all about? Isn't that what fascinates us? Isn't Hollywood a larger-than-life world, a glittering illusion created out of a need to be entertained, to be given a slice of life not as it always is but usually how we think it should be?

It's a different place from what it was. That we've seen in preceding chapters. But it remains a manufactured world of glamour and tinsel, of beautiful people, of daring love affairs and of big business. But with all that goes the greed and lust and jealousy that can produce catastrophic results for its select community. That's why we can't really close the Hollywood murder casebook completely because as long as there is a Hollywood – that institution, that symbol of American film-making, that Mecca of motion pictures that personifies every-thing one imagines the industry to be built upon – there will always be the kind of tragic consequences found within these pages.

Bibliography, Sources and Appreciation

This book is not so much the 'result' but rather a 'side effect' of some ten years of prying into the careers and private lives of movie stars and tracing the history of the Hollywood Star System, and there must be few books on the cinema which I have not scoured. It would, of course, be quite impractical to list every one of those books, not least because space would prohibit it. Also, there are many titles and authors' names of books which may have provided me with invaluable source material but which I'm unable to recall. However, I have endeavoured to compile a useful list of books, many of which proved more than helpful to me, others of which may simply be of interest if anyone should wish to pursue the lives and careers of those who have been mentioned in the pages of this book.

Anger, Kenneth, *Hollywood Babylon*, Straight Arrow Books (San Francisco), 1975

Brownlow, Kevin and Kobal, John, *Hollywood*, William Collins (London), 1979

Chaplin, Charles, *My Autobiography*, Simon & Schuster (New York), Bodley Head (London), 1964

Dennis, Felix and Atyeo, Don, *Bruce Lee–King of Kung-Fu*, Wildwood House (London), 1974

Drinkwater, John, *The Life and Adventures of Carl Laemmle*, Heinemann (New York), 1931

Eells, George, *Hedda and Louella*, Putnam (New York), 1968

Geisler, Jerry, *The Jerry Geisler Story* (as told to Pete Martin), Simon & Schuster (New York), 1960

Gifford, Denis, *Chaplin*, Doubleday (New York), 1974

Guiles, Fred Lawrence, *Marion Davies*, McGraw-Hill (New York), W.H. Allen (London), 1972

—— *Norma Jean: The Life of Marilyn Monroe*, McGraw-Hill (New York), W.H. Allen (London), 1969

Herndon, Booton, *Mary Pickford and Douglas Fairbanks*, W.H. Allen (London), 1978

Huff, Theodore, *Charlie Chaplin*, Schuman (New York), 1951

Katz, Ephraim, *The International Film Encyclopedia*, Macmillan (London), 1980

Kiernan, Thomas, *Repulsion, The Life and Times of Roman Polanski*, Grove Press (New York), New English Library (London), 1981

Lahue, Kalton C. and Brewer, Terry, *Mack Sennett's Keystone: The Man, the Myth and the Comedies*, A.S. Barnes (New York), Thomas Yoseloff Ltd (London), 1971

Lee, Linda, *The Life and Tragic Death of Bruce Lee*, W.H. Allen (London), 1975

Manvell, Roger, *Charles Chaplin*, Little Brown (Boston), 1974

McCabe, John, *Charlie Chaplin*, Robson Books (London) 1978

Niven, David, *Bring On The Empty Horses*, Putnam (New York), Hamish Hamilton (London), 1975

Niver, Kemp, *Mary Pickford, Comedienne*, Locare (Los Angeles), 1969

Pickford, Mary, *Sunshine and Shadow*, Doubleday (New York), 1955

Sciacca, Tony, *Who Killed Marilyn?*, Manor Books Inc. (New York), 1976

Sennett, Mack, *King of Comedy* (as told to Cameron Shipp), Doubleday (New York), Peter Davies (London), 1954

Shipman, David, *The Great Movie Stars: The Golden Years*, Hamlyn (London), 1970

St. Johns, Adela Rogers, *The Honeycomb*, Doubleday (New York), 1969

Stuart, Ray, *Immortals of the Screen*, Sherbourne Press (Los Angeles), Spring Books (London), 1967

Valentino, Lou, *The Films of Lana Turner*, Citadel (New Jersey), 1979

Winkler, John, *William Randolph Hearst*, The Hearst Corp. (New York), 1955

Yallop, David A., *The Day the Laughter Stopped*, St Martin's Press (New York), Hodder and Stoughton Ltd (London), 1976

Zierold, Norman, *The Hollywood Tycoons*, Coward-McCann

(New York), and published as *The Moguls* by Hamish
Hamilton (London), 1969
Zukor, Adolph, with Kraner, Dale, *The Public Is Never Wrong*,
G.P. Putnam's Sons (New York), 1953

Simply compiling the mountains of information I had was not
the point of this exercise in relating certain events from
Hollywood's past and present. To breathe life into any history,
you need some colour, and for that I drew heavily on many of
the interviews that I've conducted with movie people over the
years, searching for the Hollywood of yesterday and today.
There are also a great many people that I've associated with
who have played vital roles in keeping the film industry alive in
the less glamorous department of movie publicity. From them
I've absorbed over the years countless tales and anecdotes about
movie actors in situations the public never sees them in; the
more candid moments. From these sources I've derived information and impressions that have, I hope, provided the colour I
was looking for. And so my appreciation goes to:

Joseph Cotten for painting a vivid portrait of the Hollywood
star system and who knew what it was like to work with Marilyn
Monroe; Bonita Granville who told me about Hollywood in the
Thirties; James Stewart who worked with Lana Turner during
the Golden Years; James Coburn who retains fond memories of
Bruce Lee; Susan George who discovered today's violent
Hollywood; Jesse Lasky Jr, whose heritage is in Hollywood
history, and his wife Pat Silver with whom he revealed a little
about Monroe; Peter Cushing who actually worked with Laurel
and Hardy; Ralph Bates, Keir Dullea and Cliff Robertson who
all had the experience of working with Lana Turner; Van
Johnson who also worked with Turner and told me of his early
days caught up in the star system; Angela Lansbury who
recalled Gig Young; Andrew McLaglen who knew John Wayne
intimately, and Mike Russell who also had one or two things to
say about John Wayne; Carroll Baker who knew and worked
with Sal Mineo; Barbara Parkins who was a friend to Sharon
Tate and Roman Polanski; Barton Turner, long-time publicist
with MGM who is an avid fan of Ramon Novarro and a silent

screen buff; my one-time colleagues in the Cinerama publicity department who experienced the charm of Gig Young; and my other friends and colleagues in the film industry and in journalism who have filled my head with countless anecdotes, all helping to breathe life into the stories in this book.